Grief

Grief

CONTEMPORARY THEORY AND THE PRACTICE OF MINISTRY

Melissa M. Kelley

Fortress Press
Minneapolis

GRIEF
Contemporary Theory and the Practice of Ministry

Cover image: Spinning Nebula © Maverick Mosaics
Cover design: Laurie Ingram
Book design: PerfecType, Nashville, Tenn.

Library of Congress Cataloging-in-Publication Data
Kelley, Melissa M., 1962-
Grief : contemporary theory and the practice of ministry / Melissa M. Kelley.
p. cm.
Includes bibliographical references and index.
ISBN 978-0-8006-9661-0 (alk. paper)
1. Church work with the bereaved. 2. Grief—Religious aspects—Christianity.
I. Title.
BV4330.K45 2010
259'.6—dc22   2009052616

14 13 12 11 10   2 3 4 5 6 7 8 9 10

Contents

Preface

SEVERAL YEARS AGO, while attending a national conference on death and grief, I went out to dinner with a friend. The restaurant manager stopped by our table to chat and asked what sort of conference brought us to the city. My friend and I looked at each other, collectively took a deep breath, and replied, "Death." The restaurant manager seemed shocked and quickly left our table. About twenty minutes later, he returned and apologized for having bolted. "I didn't know what to say to people attending a conference on death," he explained, adding, "I know how to talk to the people at the next table. They are here for a conference on window curtains." Then he went on to tell us that a close family member had died a few months earlier, and he shared a bit of what his journey of grief had been like.

This incident reflects two reasons for writing this book. First, grief is all around us—a thread that connects all of humanity. It is only a matter of time before everyone in ministry will be called to respond to another in grief. Sometimes we may feel comfortable entering into this experience with others, and other times we may not. Like the restaurant manager, we may even feel tempted to bolt when the topic of death or grief comes up. And this is the second reason for this book. I believe that pastoral grief care is critical, challenging, and privileged work. People in grief are often at their most vulnerable, and we must be able to engage with and respond to them in informed, sensitive, and compassionate ways. I hope this book, which bridges contemporary grief theory and ministerial practice, helps us do just that.

    I wish to express my great gratitude to all who have supported and assisted me in the writing of this book. I am especially indebted to all who over many years have shared with me their stories of loss and grief. These stories have moved me deeply. Thanks to the Wabash Center for Teaching and Learning in Theology and Religion in Crawfordsville, Indiana, for providing a generous writing fellowship. I am indebted to colleagues at Weston Jesuit School of Theology in Cambridge, Massachusetts, and at the Boston College School of Theology and Ministry, particularly Francine Cardman, Christopher Frechette, S.J., Meg Guider, O.S.F., and John Stachniewicz. I am grateful to other friends and colleagues who have read and commented on some or all of the manuscript, particularly Elizabeth Keene, Chris Loughlin, O.P., Paula Norbert, and Kenneth Pargament. Merle Jordan of Boston University has been an extraordinary consultant and incarnates what I believe it means to be truly pastoral. Jennifer Grieco was a terrific research assistant. The book is stronger because of the thoughtful feedback and creative insights of students in my courses. I am deeply grateful for the support of my family and of good friends, especially Mary Hehir and Mer Zovko. Rolf Jacobson of Luther Seminary introduced me to the wonderful people at Fortress Press. Susan Johnson of Fortress Press has been a most creative and calming editor. And my deepest love and gratitude go to my husband, Allen Fairfax, for his faithful and patient support, good cheer, and loving kindness. Thank you.

Introduction

MILLIE IS A sixty-three-year-old Caucasian woman whose husband, George, died five months ago. Millie has had a sometimes harrowing life, including physical abuse and neglect as a child and removal from her family. Millie's first husband was physically and verbally abusive to her. Her second husband, George, was a kinder man, although their marriage was emotionally distant. At fifty-two, Millie decided to pursue a lifelong dream of teaching, and George supported her in this. When George became ill, a part of Millie resented having to leave her teaching job to take care of him, and she felt some relief when he died. But now the full reality of his death is hitting her. She is in terrible financial straits and may lose her home. She is not sleeping or eating well. She has had disturbing dreams in which she feels visited by George, who chastises her for feeling relief when he died. Millie feels like her life is falling apart, and she doesn't know what it all means. She is confused and terrified about her future.

Millie has struggled all her life to feel any sort of secure or loving connection to God. She feels that God was not with her when her parents abused her and she was taken away. God was not with her when she was moved from foster family to foster family. She has made her way in the world without any help from God. Millie says the closest she has ever come to naming her experience of God is the Bible story about the shepherd who leaves the ninety-nine sheep to find the one that has wandered off. She is the one that has wandered off, but in her experience, the shepherd has never come to find her. Millie occasionally goes to church, and sometimes she finds the prayers and music comforting. She has not been to church since George's funeral.

Robert is a thirty-eight-year-old African American man who has been married to Grace for eleven years. He is pursuing a divinity degree as preparation for ordination. Robert and Grace tried to have a child for eight years, and they rejoiced when Desirée was born. Almost immediately, however, Desirée began to have health problems, and she died at three months of age. Robert and Grace were devastated. They turned to their community of friends, family, and church to hold them up. Robert experienced a crisis of faith as he realized that the theology he had embraced up to that point did not help him in his devastation. For many months, all he could do was to pray the psalms of lament and to rail against God. Robert felt that he had to let God know exactly how he was feeling. He also questioned whether he could be a minister and deal with people's horrible losses. Very gradually, over the past year and a half, Robert has begun to feel that he can now be a more compassionate minister because of his own heartbreak and devastation. With the help of their church community, Robert and Grace have established a scholarship fund in Desirée's memory. Recently, Robert and Grace have begun to talk again about creating a family.

What is grief? As these two vignettes demonstrate, grief can look and feel very different for different people. Millie and Robert have both suffered major losses, but they are not responding in identical ways. Their experiences of grief are particular, complex, intricate, and multidimensional.

The experience of grief has been a source of intrigue and curiosity throughout history, and it continues to stimulate thought and theory in various fields, such as theology, psychology, sociology, anthropology, and medicine. Unfortunately, while so many fields are concerned with grief and with those who are grieving, these fields tend to function in isolation from each other. A striking example of this phenomenon is the substantial disconnection that exists between the world of ministry and the secular world of grief research, theory, and care.

In the secular arena of grief research, theory, and care, our understanding of the experience of grief is evolving, and the last twenty years or so have constituted a virtual quantum leap in this evolution. Secular grief researchers, theorists, and clinicians have revisited and challenged many long-accepted and even petrified dimensions of traditional grief theory. For example, many contemporary grief theorists have critiqued the concept of "stages of grief" as inaccurate, seriously limited, and unhelpful. Proposals of stages or phases of grieving suggest an invariant universality of human experience that neglects individual, familial, societal, cultural, and contextual factors. In contrast to some of the limiting and prescriptive "stage" talk, some contemporary theorists describe the affirmation and/or reconstruction of meaning after loss as the "central process in grieving" (Neimeyer 1999, 67).[1] Also, in contrast to the long-standing psychoanalytic understanding of grief as requiring the total *decathexis*—that is, withdrawal of emotional energy—from the deceased person, some current theorists and clinicians describe the natural place of continuing bonds with the deceased in the ongoing lives of many grieving people (Klass, Silverman, & Nickman 1996). Such new and creative work has revolutionized the secular field of grief theory and care.

Although ministers are very often on the front lines of caring for those who are grieving, they sometimes do not have access to such contemporary theory and research to inform their care. For example, recent research has delineated five specific trajectories that grief seemed to follow in one population; this research has clear implications for who may need help with their grieving and who may be likely to move through their grief with resilience and hope (Boerner, Wortman, & Bonanno 2005). Ministers without regular access to cutting-edge research may not know about these trajectories and the possible implications for appropriate pastoral and spiritual care.

At the same time, ministers are deeply concerned with the religious, theological, spiritual, and pastoral dimensions of the grief experience. These areas are seldom addressed in the secular grief field at large. For example, national surveys consistently reveal that close to 90 percent of the U.S. population describe themselves as religious or spiritual (Miller 2007a). Yet in the indices of two recent handbooks on grief written by some of the world's foremost theorists and published by the American Psychological

Association (Stroebe, Hansson, Schut, & Stroebe 2008; Stroebe, Hansson, Stroebe, & Schut 2001a), there is not a single reference to God.

In light of this serious and unhelpful disconnection between the secular and ministerial worlds in the area of grief, the goal of this book is twofold. First, I hope to offer ministers the most up-to-date theory and research in grief to inform their care of others. They and the people for whom they care deserve nothing less. But this theory and research should not stand in isolation. If it cannot be integrated with the religious, theological, and pastoral paradigms out of which ministers work, it is of limited value. Therefore, my second goal is to model a significant integration of this contemporary theory and research with important religious, theological, and ministerial perspectives.

In exploring any field that can be highly theoretical and abstract, I find metaphors helpful. Metaphors offer us a way of connecting words and ideas with images, concrete matters, real life. I find the metaphor of *mosaic* helpful and expansive in considering grief, and I propose that in many important ways grief is like a mosaic. Throughout this book, I will develop the metaphor of *the mosaic of grief*. Of course, no metaphor is perfect or complete, and slavish adherence to a metaphor may eventually lead to distortion or force fitting of one's ideas. Also, I do not mean to trivialize or romanticize grief by equating it with a work of mosaic art. There is nothing romantic about deep pain and agonizing loss. I keep these cautions firmly in mind as I offer some introductory thoughts about mosaics and about the mosaic of grief.

Mosaic as Art Form

Mosaic is an art form that is both ancient and contemporary. Early mosaic remains date back to several centuries before the birth of Jesus, and today artists around the world continue to craft mosaics. Mosaics are formed by the combination and arrangement of multiple small pieces or fragments of material, called *tesserae*. The tesserae may be made of glass, tile, ceramic, marble, or gemstones. Some mosaicists also work with discarded materials, such as broken pottery pieces or shards of china. The particular combination of these individual pieces forms a whole, the mosaic.

The spaces between the tesserae are called *interstices*, and the interstices are a significant part of the overall design of the mosaic. That is, what is *not* there is as significant as what *is* there in the formation of the whole. Sometimes, the eye of the observer may be drawn more to the interstices than to the tesserae.

Every mosaic is unique because of the many particular features that comprise a mosaic. For example, some mosaics are thematic and seem to present something of a coherent story. Others depict specific figures, such as people or animals, in vivid detail. Other mosaics are largely abstract and invite the eye simply to wander over them. With the particular arrangement of the tesserae, some mosaics convey shadow and depth. Others seem rather flat and one-dimensional. Some mosaics suggest flow or movement, known as *andamento*, such as that of a river winding its way through the work. Others seem static. Some mosaics do not seem to have a pattern or design when seen up close. However, as with an impressionist painting, a pattern emerges as one steps back from the mosaic.

The colors used in mosaics are endlessly variegated. Some tesserae beautifully reflect or refract light. Some are laced with dazzling gold or silver. Others are opaque or muted. Some have rich undertones. Others are clear or shiny. Some seem to take on new and unexpected shades because of the colors of the surrounding tesserae.

Mosaic art is difficult and painstaking. So many elements must be integrated, such as material, color, placement, and pattern. The mosaicist may intend one pattern, only to discover that an unexpected pattern emerges due to the many variables in this art form. Some say this art is not for the faint of heart. And yet mosaics are among the most beautiful and enduring artistic creations of all.

Mosaic as a Metaphor for Grief

How is grief like a mosaic? At this early point, I would like to suggest two initial aspects of this metaphor. First, as no two mosaics can ever be exactly the same, so no two experiences of grief are the same. As each mosaic is particular, fashioned by many individual elements configured in unique ways, so each person's experience of grief is particular. It is formed by the unique interplay of all aspects of one's life—one's past, one's relationships, one's ways of making meaning, one's experience of the Divine, one's history of losses, one's sense of community, one's cultural perspectives, and so on. Let's recall the two vignettes from the beginning of this chapter. Both Millie and Robert have experienced significant loss, and each is grieving. However, their experiences of grief look quite different. Each is fashioning an intricate mosaic of his or her own.

In order to begin to imagine a particular mosaic, such as that of Millie or Robert, we might ponder questions such as these: How secure and safe were their relationships to important people as they were growing up? How secure and safe are their relationships in adulthood? How do they experience their relationship with God? What is their history of various losses? How have they found or made meaning following these losses? How do they understand God's role in their suffering? How have they kept going in their grief, and how helpful have religion and religious community been? How are they remembering or connecting with their deceased loved one now? How hopeful do they feel about their future? All of these dimensions of life, and many more, may be constitutive parts of the mosaic of grief.

While no two mosaics are the same, there is still much we can learn about mosaic art in general, some of which I have introduced above. Likewise, while we must keep the particularity of one's grief always before us, this does not mean that there is nothing we can say about grief in general. This is the second aspect of the mosaic of grief that I would like to propose at this point. It is important to learn what we can about the general elements and forms of grief, balancing this learning with an honoring of the particular.[2] If we are limited in our understanding of grief, we risk seeing only part of the mosaic. We risk seeing some colors and not others. We risk seeing flatness where there is fullness and form, like trying to watch a 3-D movie without the special glasses. We risk seeing interstices or gaps that are in fact not there. The great risk is seeing another's mosaic of grief in only partial, limited, or incomplete ways. And this often means that the care one offers is partial, limited, or incomplete.

Description of Terms

This book is also a mosaic. It is made up of the pieces about grief that I think are critical, arranged in a particular way. There are gaps, some because of what we do not yet know about the experience of grief, others due to my own limitations of perspective. Each chapter will add to the color, pattern, and intricacy of the whole. As the mosaic of this book emerges, I hope it offers a fuller understanding of the human experience of grief than either ministerial or secular perspectives alone can offer. I begin by addressing how I understand and use key terms throughout the book.

Types of Loss

The vast majority of work done on grief has been with reference to the grief following a death. While death of a significant other is clearly an important and often life-changing experience of grief, we also know that death is not the only loss that can prompt grief. In their classic work *All Our Losses, All Our Griefs*, pastoral writers Kenneth Mitchell and Herbert Anderson expand the discussion of grief by positing that "unless we understand that all losses, even 'minor' ones, give rise to grief, we shall misunderstand its fundamental nature. . . . Loss, not death, is the normative metaphor for understanding those experiences in human life that produce grief" (1983, 18–19). They then offer six categories of loss that may prompt grief; any single experience of loss may touch on one or more of these categories:

1. *Material* loss refers to the loss of actual physical matters, such as a prized possession or one's childhood home.
2. *Role* loss refers to the loss of a familiar role or function, such as that of competent manager after retirement or that of spouse after a divorce.
3. *Relationship* loss refers to the loss of a particular way of relating with another or others, such as with colleagues after a job layoff or with one's parent who is in physical or mental decline.
4. *Systemic* loss refers to loss that an entire group or system experiences, such as what city dwellers may experience when an

important landmark is torn down or what an office staff experiences when a colleague moves.

5. *Functional* loss refers to the loss of use or functioning of a part of one's body, such as loss of mobility following a paralyzing accident or the slow deterioration of one's vision as one ages.

6. *Intrapsychic* loss refers to the loss within one's own psyche of a way of thinking about oneself, one's future, or the world, such as a painful recognition of one's limitations or the abandonment of a lifelong dream.

While much of the discussion in this book focuses on the grief following a significant death, I hope readers will also be able to draw connections to the many other life experiences that can prompt grief.

Bereavement

Some researchers use the terms *grief* and *bereavement* essentially interchangeably. I find it helpful to distinguish between these terms. *Bereavement*, as defined by psychiatrists Harold Kaplan, Benjamin Sadock, and Jack Grebb, "literally means the state of being deprived of someone by death" (1994, 80). In this book, the term *bereavement* is used to describe this actual state of deprivation or loss, without presumption of any particular response. That is, one may be bereaved without necessarily experiencing grief.

Grief

In this book, the term *grief* is understood as one's response to an important loss. This response is sometimes marked by "severe and prolonged distress" (Weiss 2001, 47), which may be manifested in various ways.

Mourning

Mourning is typically understood as the psychoanalytic term for grieving. It also refers to "the societal expression of postbereavement behavior and practices" (Kaplan, Sadock, & Grebb 1994, 80), which are often prescribed socially or culturally. In this book I will generally refer to *grief* rather than *mourning*. When the term *mourning* is used, it is understood as largely synonymous with *grief*.

Minister

This book is written primarily for those who minister to others in times of grief. This includes those who are ordained, preparing for ordination, or preparing for ministry as lay church leaders. This book is also written for other religious professionals, pastoral counselors, spiritual directors, and spiritually oriented psychotherapists. Finally, it is written for interested relatives and friends of those in grief. For the most part, I will use *minister* to refer to all of these groups of people. In a fundamental sense, in tending to others in need, all are truly ministering. I hope that this book will assist all who minister to offer compassionate, substantive care to those who are grieving.

1

Contemporary
Topics in Grief

THE GRIEF FIELD has evolved and grown dramatically over the last two decades, and many recent developments in grief research and theory are highly relevant to ministry. In this chapter we will look more closely at some possible sources, manifestations, and features of grief that ministers need to be aware of and sensitive to when offering care to people who grieve. We begin with three possible dimensions of the grief experience that often are not recognized: disenfranchised grief, chronic sorrow, and grief born of injustice.

Three Dimensions of Grief

Disenfranchised Grief

As measured by our responses, we can say that all losses are not created equal. We pay more attention to some losses than to others. And some losses never make it onto our radar screen at all. Given our limitations as humans and the vast scope of loss on the contemporary global scene, it cannot be any other way. For each of us, the losses that we notice and those that we don't are particular, based on such factors as our geographic location, our histories, our cultures, our perspectives, and our values. Some losses may be neglected or ignored not only by individuals but also by entire groups, societies, or cultures. Author and professor of gerontology Kenneth Doka (1989, 2002, 2008) has offered the contemporary grief field the important concept of *disenfranchised grief*. Grief that is disenfranchised is "not openly acknowledged, socially validated, or publicly observed" (Doka 2002, 5). That is, there is no public or social acknowledgment of or support for one's grief or even one's "right to grieve" (Doka 2008, 225).

Doka suggests possible causes of such disenfranchisement. First, it may be due to how one grieves. For example, in a culturally diverse setting, one group may not understand how another person or group expresses grief and therefore assumes there is no grief or need for support. Another cause of disenfranchised grief is the sort of loss one has experienced. Even today losses related to pregnancy and childbirth, such as infertility, miscarriage, and stillbirth, are not always recognized as devastating losses for many, and therefore support for the grieving is not forthcoming. Sometimes the circumstances of a loss lead to disenfranchisement. When a death is due to suicide, survivors may not disclose the facts of the death, fearing judgment or stigma; their particular grief may then be disenfranchised.

Another cause of disenfranchised grief, according to Doka, may be the type of relationship that was lost. A gay person whose life partner has died may receive little acknowledgement or support from his or her faith community. This may be because the community did not approve of their homosexual relationship. It may also be that, fearing the community's disapproval or rejection, the partners never acknowledged the true depth of their connection and so others do not know what has been lost. Also, when a death occurs, attention usually focuses on the surviving spouse, children, and parents, while friends of the deceased may feel disenfranchised in their grief. The grief of siblings, for whom the death may be profoundly painful, may also be neglected or ignored (Miller 2008c; Wray 2003).

By depriving people of the acknowledgment and support they most need in their time of loss, the disenfranchisement of grief may create additional grief and pain, which also may be disenfranchised (Doka 2008; Kuhn 2002). Ministers and faith communities have a particular responsibility to ensure that no grieving persons in their midst go unrecognized and unsupported. In Matthew 5:4, we hear Jesus' all-embracing words of solace, "Blessed are those who mourn, for they will be comforted." Jesus did not single out certain groups of mourners as deserving comfort. He blessed all those who grieve. As the hands and feet of Christ on earth, so must we do. In order not to disenfranchise the grief of others, we must regularly ask ourselves these critical questions: Whose losses do we notice? Whose grief do we support? Whose grief might we ignore, invalidate, or minimize?

Chronic Sorrow

Some people experience losses that are ongoing, and these people may therefore experience ongoing or chronic sorrow. *Chronic sorrow* is a concept first introduced and developed by rehabilitation counselor Simon Olshansky (cited in Roos 2002) to describe the grief of parents of a child diagnosed with a serious developmental disability, such as mental retardation. For many parents, the child's disability constituted the loss of their fantasy of how their child would be and what parenting would be like. This was a "living loss" (Roos 2002, xv), since the child was alive and in need of ongoing care; for many parents, their grief or sorrow was therefore also ongoing.

Many people endure living losses. Family members of those with chronic mental illness may live with a lifetime of related losses, such as loss of the relationship that might have been if the person did not have mental illness, and loss of a freer life without the constant strain of worry and caregiving. A contemporary source of living losses is the wars in Iraq and Afghanistan. Due to excellent and immediate medical care and better protective equipment, many military personnel are surviving injuries that likely would have killed them in prior wars (Doll & Bowley 2008; Hoge et al. 2008). What this means in some instances is that men and women are returning to their families with severe and life-changing injuries, with which all parties must then cope. And by some estimates, as many as 25 percent of veterans of these wars report mental health struggles when they return home (Miller 2008a). For some people, such changes to their lives and expectations for the future may constitute a living loss.

Researcher and educator Pauline Boss points out that some ongoing losses are not clearly defined but rather are ambiguous, meaning they are "incomplete or uncertain" (Boss 1999a, 3). Families of kidnapped children or soldiers missing in action must live, sometimes for decades, without any clear knowledge of where their loved ones are or even whether they are still alive. Relatives of someone with Alzheimer's disease might struggle with what Boss calls the "psychological absence" (Boss 1999a, 45) of the person, despite the person's physical presence. With ambiguous loss, people may not know if or when they should grieve, or even what exactly they are grieving. As Boss suggests, "The certainty we hunger for in human relationships is most poignantly unachievable when a person we care about [is] neither clearly absent nor clearly present in our lives" (Boss 1999b, 4).

Psychotherapist Susan Roos proposes that people facing all sorts of living losses may experience the pain and challenge of chronic sorrow:

> Chronic sorrow is about years upon years of living with the inevitability of loss, of continually negotiating reality demands required by the loss, and of contending with ongoing and resurgent grief responses. . . . Central to chronic sorrow is the role of fantasy—of what could have been or should have been (and maybe will be, after all). Activation of the fantasy intensifies painful emotions, as the disparity between the fantasy and current living reality can be cruel and wounding. (2002, 27)

According to Roos, there is some evidence that chronic sorrow may be on the rise, perhaps due in part to medical advances that allow people to survive traumatic injuries and to live longer with debilitating physical conditions. Therefore, ministers must be sensitive to the possible presence of chronic sorrow among those for whom they care. In the Gospel of Mark, a man asks Jesus to heal his son who has been possessed by a destructive spirit for many years. In a beautifully touching moment, Jesus asks the father, "How long has this been happening to him?" to which the father replies, "From childhood" (Mark 9:21). Jesus seems to care deeply about the long suffering of both the boy and his father, and he brings healing to the family. So we, too, are called to care deeply about those who suffer living losses and chronic sorrow.

Grief Born of Injustice

A critical area of grief about which ministers must be aware is what I call *grief born of injustice*. For natural reasons, the almost exclusive emphasis in both secular and pastoral grief care is responding to grievers once a loss has occurred. But as we know well, much grief never needed to happen in the first place. It is the result of injustice. By grief born of injustice, I mean the following: it is grief due in whole or in part to injustice. It is grief that is caused by unjust structures and/or by unjust actions or inactions of individuals, groups, and systems. It is grief that is not part of the "natural order" of things. It is grief that did not need to happen. It is grief that was preventable.

Perhaps the most stunning occurrence of the grief born of injustice is related to global poverty. According to the World Bank, 1.4 billion people live in extreme poverty (less than $1.25 a day), while close to 2.6 billion people survive on less than two dollars a day.[1] As many as 155 million people were pushed into poverty between 2007 and 2009 due to soaring global food prices.[2] While worldwide food production is sufficient for feeding the world's population (Smith 2006), someone dies of starvation every 3.6 seconds; the majority of these are children under five.[3] Every year, waterborne diseases such as dysentery and cholera kill five million people, most of them children, and more than one billion people do not have a source of safe drinking water.[4] Sadly, we could go on and on. In the wake of all of this suffering and death, countless people grieve. This grieving is a direct consequence of injustice.

Because this area is largely neglected in the grief world, we know little about the possible features and costs of the grief born of injustice. For example, how does this experience shape a survivor's sense of self, sense of the world, and sense of God? Watching a loved one suffer or die due to injustice, some people may question God's role in this suffering or feel abandoned by God in their grief. They may resonate with the words of the psalmist: "For you are the God in whom I take refuge; why have you cast me off? Why must I walk about mournfully because of the oppression of the enemy?" (Ps. 43:2).

The grief born of injustice demands much of the minister. At the most immediate level, when we care for those who grieve because of injustice, we offer comfort. We attend to them; we notice their suffering; we acknowledge the cause(s); we do not disenfranchise their grief. And critically, we make clear that God, too, sees their suffering and cares deeply for them. "From oppression and violence he redeems their life; and precious is their blood in his sight" (Ps. 72:14). I believe we are called to respond in another way also. While caring for grieving individuals or communities is essential, we must do what we can to prevent the grief born of injustice in the first place. Comfort after the fact may be of questionable consolation to someone whose grief was preventable. We must understand grief care as sometimes encompassing both pastoral response and prophetic action. Our efforts to balance both, while so very challenging, are necessary to address the grief born of injustice.

The Trajectories of Grief

Traditional understandings of grief have often defined the grief experience in overly narrow ways. For instance, researchers have frequently maintained that there are three primary patterns of grief. The first, called *common* grief, is marked by an initial increase in distress following a death; this distress abates slowly with time. The second pattern, *chronic grief*, is marked by high distress following a death, and this distress remains high over time. And the third pattern, *delayed grief*, is marked by low distress after a death, with a rise in distress at some later point (Bonanno et al. 2002). Important new research is helping us to assess and challenge these assumptions regarding three basic grief patterns. In one study, people's grief experiences could be sorted into five patterns or *trajectories* (Bonanno et al. 2002; Bonanno, Wortman, & Nesse 2004; Boerner, Wortman, & Bonanno 2005). Of course, we cannot extrapolate too widely from findings drawn from one sample population. At the same time, these findings help us to understand that there may be many patterns of grief, with important implications for care.

The research by George Bonanno, Kathrin Boerner, and colleagues on the trajectories of grief involved a sample of English-speaking older married couples (where the husband was at least sixty-five years old) in the Detroit area. Over the course of the study, some of the participants died, and the researchers examined the grief of the surviving spouses.

Importantly, the researchers began to get to know the participants an average of *three years* before the spouses died. They also followed the participants for *four years* after the death, interviewing the widowed spouses six months, eighteen months, and forty-eight months postloss. Before and/or after the death, the researchers inquired about matters such as what the marriage was like, whether the spouse had been ill before dying, whether the survivor had experienced strain in caring for the spouse, how much support the survivor received from others before and after the death, whether the survivor felt he or she had benefited in any way from being widowed (e.g., becoming stronger by learning to do more for oneself), how well the survivor felt he or she was coping, level of depression, level of grief (e.g., thinking a lot about and yearning for the deceased), how much he or she accepted the death before the loss, and to what degree the survivor felt that the world was basically just.

Over the course of the study, the researchers were able to differentiate five trajectories of response to the loss, which are shown in the diagram on p. 18. On the left-hand side of the chart, we see that the researchers were assessing the depression of the participants. It is important to note that grief and depression are not the same thing. Not everyone who is grieving experiences depression, and not everyone who is depressed is grieving. However, there is often significant overlap between depression and grief, at least initially, and that was the case with this sample; patterns of grief and patterns of depression were similar. Across the bottom of the chart, we see the measurement of time; we are looking at people's depression before the death happened (preloss) and then six months, eighteen months, and forty-eight months after the death. At the forty-eight-month mark, there were ninety-two people in the study; 90 percent were women, with an average age of seventy (Boerner, Wortman, and Bonanno 2005). After differentiating these five trajectories, the researchers were able to draw on both the prospective data and the data gathered at the various intervals to shape an understanding of the grief experience of those on each trajectory. Let us now consider each trajectory.

The first trajectory is *chronic depression*. As the chart indicates, the people on this trajectory (9.8 percent of the sample) had very high depression before the death occurred. By six months postloss, their depression had

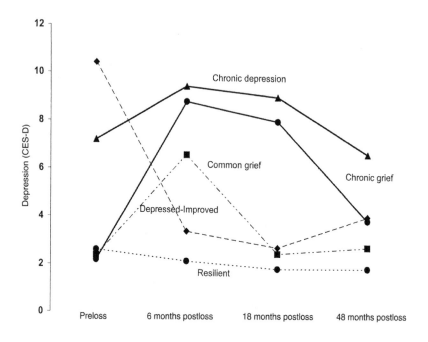

The Trajectories of Grief from Boerner, Wortman, & Bonano 2005 (N=92)

increased and then began to lessen gradually. Importantly, this group had the highest depression scores at forty-eight months postloss. The participants whose grief followed this trajectory tended to have certain things in common. They were rather negative about their marriages and their spouses, and they derived the least comfort from positive memories of their spouses. At the same time, they demonstrated very high interpersonal dependency, both on their spouses and in general. They found widowhood quite difficult and they did not see themselves as coping well. They received low support. These participants also described a belief in the "uncontrollability of negative events" (Bonanno et al. 2002, 1159) and had the greatest struggle with meaning. Overall, their adjustment to the death seemed most problematic. In considering all these factors, including the participants' very high depression preloss, the researchers suggested that those on this trajectory may have been struggling with emotional difficulties before the loss, and these difficulties were then exacerbated by the deaths of their spouses (Bonanno, Wortman, & Nesse 2004).

The second trajectory is *chronic grief*. We can see that the preloss depression of people on this trajectory (10.9 percent of the sample) was low; their depression then spiked by six months postloss and was still high at eighteen months postloss. By forty-eight months postloss, it had come down significantly but was still higher than it was before the death. Thus, this is a portrait of a long and difficult grief experience. Those whose grief followed this trajectory tended to have certain things in common. They described their marriages very positively, and they were also highly dependent on their spouses and in general. Their spouses were more likely to have been healthy before dying, and they experienced low strain as caregivers for their spouses. They had low support, and they also saw themselves as poor copers. After the death, they experienced high yearning and emotional pangs, thought a lot about the death, and searched for meaning. They expressed the most regret about their married relationship. In considering all these factors, the researchers suggested that those on this trajectory may have experienced significant and lasting turmoil because they lost a healthy spouse (i.e., the death may have been unexpected) on whom they were highly dependent (Bonanno, Wortman, & Nesse 2004).

The third trajectory is *common grief*. The people on this trajectory had very low depression before the loss. Their depression then peaked at six months postloss, came down steadily by eighteen months postloss, and was rather low at forty-eight months postloss. Interestingly, the common grief trajectory—named for what has traditionally been understood as the most common pattern of grief—captured only 10.9 percent of the sample. Those whose grief followed this trajectory tended to have certain things in common. At the six-month mark, they derived high comfort from their positive memories of their spouses. Their spouses had been seriously ill before dying, although the survivors did not provide direct care during the illness. They had good coping abilities, and they saw some benefits to their widowhood.

The fourth trajectory is *depressed-improved*. We can see that those on this trajectory (18.5 percent of the sample) had the highest depression before the death. Their depression then plummeted by six months postloss and was still low at eighteen months postloss. By forty-eight months postloss, their depression was starting to tick up a bit again, demonstrating a "trend" in the direction of "adjustment problems over time" (Boerner, Wortman, & Bonanno 2005, 71). The researchers had many questions about this trajectory. Why would one's depression plummet after a death and stay rather low? Were these people in unhappy marriages? Was the strain of caregiving taking a terrible toll, and therefore the death constituted a relief of sorts? Those whose grief followed this trajectory tended to have certain things in common. They were low in dependency both on their spouses and in general, took pride in their coping ability, and experienced some benefits of widowhood. Importantly, they were the most negative and most ambivalent about both their spouses and their marriages. Their spouses were ill before dying, and they received low support; therefore, the death of their spouses may have constituted "the end of a chronic stressor" (Bonanno, Wortman, & Nesse 2004, 268). Also, they struggled with some emotional instability, were somewhat neurotic, and "believed strongly that the world was particularly unjust to them" (ibid., 261). The fact that their depression seemed to be ticking up again at forty-eight months postloss was of concern. The researchers hypothesized that "subsequent depression may emerge after a period of well-being in those cases in which people are required to perform stressful caregiving duties for a spouse for whom they have negative or ambivalent feelings" (Boerner, Wortman, & Bonanno 2005, 72).

And the fifth trajectory is *resilient*. Those on this trajectory had very low depression before the loss, and their depression remained low right through forty-eight months postloss. Interestingly, this trajectory reflected a full 50 percent of the sample. Researchers had questions about the people on this trajectory. Was their "resilience" really an indication of delayed grief? Were they not terribly attached to their spouses in the first place, and is that why they experienced such low distress over time? Those people whose grief followed the *resilient* trajectory tended to have certain things in common. They had been married forty-four years on average and described their marriages as satisfying for the most part. They were not colder or more avoidant and actually derived the most comfort over time from positive memories of the deceased. They demonstrated low dependency and good coping. Before the death, they had the highest support, were more accepting of death, and described a greater belief in a just world. After the death, they had the fewest regrets, low yearning, low emotional pangs, and low search for meaning. This did not mean they experienced no grief, however; "the majority *did* report experiencing at least some yearning and emotional pangs during the first 6 months of bereavement, and virtually all respondents reported at least some grief-related intrusion and rumination" (Bonanno, Wortman, & Neese 2004, 268). Thus, their resilience did not seem evidence of "delayed" grief; rather, it seemed to reflect emotional stability and adaptive adjustment.

Of course, there are limitations to this research (e.g., small sample size, not diverse in terms of age, gender, and culture/language). Nevertheless, the work on the trajectories of grief is helpful to ministers in at least three ways. First, it makes clear that, for many people, grief and its associated distress may endure for years after a death. We must consider how we and the faith community might acknowledge, ask about, pray for, and ritualize people's losses in an ongoing way. Second, for this sample, the grief journey unfolded in numerous and varied patterns. These findings may help us challenge our assumptions about how grief ought to unfold and bring a more nuanced sensitivity to the grief experiences of others. With this understanding, we can tailor our responses appropriately. For example, the researchers suggest that those enduring chronic depression may benefit from attention to their ongoing emotional struggles, while chronic grievers, who were extremely dependent on their spouses, may benefit from attention to the enormity of their loss and the need to shape a new sense of self (Boerner, Wortman, & Bonanno 2005). Third, this research may help us anticipate one's possible grief trajectory by noting such things as the sort of support one receives before a death and how one assesses one's own coping ability. We may even create additional support for those who seem particularly vulnerable to an especially difficult grief experience.

Central Features of the Grieving Process

When a loss has happened, what does grieving then entail? Among the contributions of contemporary grief theory are two insights into the experience of grieving that are little addressed by traditional grief theory. One relates to coping with loss; the other concerns continuity of relationship with the deceased.

The Dual Process Model of Coping

When any sort of stressful event happens, people must somehow cope with it. There are numerous theories and models of how people cope with the stress of bereavement.[5] Informed by many of these theories and models and in considering the death of a partner, bereavement research- ers Margaret Stroebe and Henk Schut (1999, 2001) have proposed the *dual process model of coping with bereavement*. According to the dual process model, bereaved people must cope with varied stressors. Some of these stressors are *loss oriented*; that is, they have to do with the loss itself. Loss- oriented stressors include thinking a lot about the circumstances of the death and yearning for the person who has died. But these are not the only stressors that bereaved people must face; they also must cope with the changes and demands of their new postloss reality. These *restoration- oriented* stressors include having to take on new roles and responsibilities in the wake of the death (e.g., assuming financial tasks that were always handled by the deceased person) and beginning new activities (e.g., a new job) or relationships.

Many traditional theories of grief have maintained that success- ful adaptation to loss demands a focus on the hard work of grief, that is, confronting the reality of the loss and working through the pain of it.[6] Stroebe and Schut concur that such loss-oriented stressors must be addressed, particularly early on, but they propose that this ought not to be done to the exclusion of the restoration-oriented stressors. In their dual process model, they propose that successful adaptation to loss requires a sort of balance in coping with the demands of both loss orientation and restoration orientation. They use the term *oscillation* to describe how one's coping efforts shift dynamically between these two orientations. "At times the bereaved will confront aspects of loss, at other times avoid them, and the same applies to the tasks of restoration. Sometimes, too, there will be 'time out,' when grieving is left alone" (Stroebe & Schut 2001, 395).

More study of the dual process model is needed; for example, how widely applicable is this model to various sorts of loss? How applicable is it to various cultures? But some preliminary research seems to suggest that those who oscillate between focusing on their loss and focusing on their changed life cope well over time (Frantz, Farrell, & Trolley 2001), whereas exclusive emphasis on "grief work" (i.e., loss orientation) might be detrimental to recovery from grief (Silver & Wortman 1980). It appears that attention to both the pain of loss and the demands of a changed life may be necessary and that "oscillation between the two enables a balanced recovery to occur" (Archer 2008, 58).

Ministers can support and encourage grieving people in this oscillation. We can help them honor and attend to both the raw pain of loss and the need to move with hope and trust into the future to which God calls them. Both loss and life must be honored and balanced, as best one can. As we support those who seek and perhaps struggle with this balance, the familiar words of Ecclesiastes may be helpful: "For everything there is a season, and a time for every matter under heaven: . . . A time to break down, and a time to build up; a time to weep, and a time to laugh; a time to mourn, and a time to dance" (Eccl. 3:1, 3b-4).

Continuing Bonds

When a loved one has died, some people struggle to understand what, if any, sort of connection they now have with the deceased person. As we will see in the next chapter on the history of grief theory, traditional (psychoanalytic) grief theory has understood the goal of mourning as the withdrawal of psychic energy from the lost loved one to make possible the reinvestment of it in new relationships. According to this theory, any sense that one continues to feel a connection to the deceased loved one may be evidence of pathology (Hagman 2001). Of course, throughout time, many people, religions, and cultures have described some sort of continuity of relationship with those who have died. For example, Japanese ancestor rituals acknowledge the important and ongoing relationship of the living with their deceased family members (Goss & Klass 2005). In Mexico, *el Día de los Muertos*, or the Day of the Dead, marks the "enduring ties between the living and the dead" (DeSpelder & Strickland 2005, 114).

I offer two other examples. In his poignant 1798 poem "We Are Seven," British poet William Wordsworth describes a child's unshakable sense of ongoing connection to her deceased siblings (Van Doren 1950, 56–58).

. . . I met a little cottage Girl:
She was eight years old, she said;
Her hair was thick with many a curl
That clustered round her head.

. . . "Sisters and brothers, little Maid,
How many may you be?"
"How many? Seven in all," she said
And wondering looked at me.

"And where are they? I pray you tell."
She answered, "Seven are we;
And two of us at Conway dwell,
And two are gone to sea.

"Two of us in the church-yard lie,
My sister and my brother;
And, in the church-yard cottage, I
Dwell near them with my mother."

. . . "You run about, my little Maid,
Your limbs they are alive;
If two are in the church-yard laid,
Then ye are only five."

"Their graves are green, they may be seen,"
The little Maid replied,
"Twelve steps or more from my mother's door,
And they are side by side.

"My stockings there I often knit.
My kerchief there I hem;
And there upon the ground I sit,
And sing a song to them.

"And often after sunset, Sir,
When it is light and fair,
I take my little porringer,
And eat my supper there."

. . . "How many are you, then," said I,
"If they two are in heaven?"

Quick was the little Maid's reply,
"O Master! we are seven."

"But they are dead; those two are dead!
Their spirits are in heaven!"
'Twas throwing words away; for still
The little Maid would have her will,
And said, "Nay, we are seven!"

A second example concerns Eleanor Roosevelt, the first lady of the United States from 1933 to 1945. Eleanor experienced much loss, particularly early in her life. Her mother died when she was eight, and her little brother died when she was nine. Eleanor was deeply attached to her inconsistent but beloved father, Elliott. He also died when she was nine but remained a very important figure in her life after his death. She wrote, "From that time on . . . I lived with him more closely, probably, than I had when he was alive" (quoted in Persico 2008, 25).

In recent years, important work has looked at the continuity of relationship with the deceased that so many people experience.[7] Researchers Dennis Klass and Phyllis Silverman and psychiatrist Steven Nickman (1996) introduced the term *continuing bonds* to describe this experience. For many people, having a sense of a continuing bond with a deceased person is not pathological but rather seems to be a source of great comfort and healing. This continuing bond can take many forms. First, the person may live on in *memory*. This may seem a rather limited source of connection, but it need not be. We revisit our memories throughout our lives, sometimes coming to new insights or realizations in the process. For instance, as we age, we may remember deceased parents when they were the same age as we are now, and we may glean new insights about our parents from these memories. This understanding may help us to feel a new or deeper sort of connection to our parents, even long after their deaths.

A second sort of continuing bond is our sense of the *legacy* that a deceased person has left; that is, the many ways they have touched us and continue to touch and influence us. And we may actively engage this legacy, inviting it to define our lives in significant ways. For instance, we may choose to continue work that was important to the deceased, or we may raise money for causes that they espoused. We may also try to emulate some of the qualities that we most loved or admired in them. In all these ways, "we blend what they have given, and continue to give, into the life histories we reshape and redirect" (Attig 2001, 51). Continuing bonds may take other forms as well. For instance, some people feel that their deceased loved ones watch over and protect them. Others continue to define themselves, at least in part, in relationship to one who has died. A father whose young child died has said, "The earthly bond with my child has been broken. . . . But in my mind and in my heart, I am her father forever" (English 2009, A6).

It is certainly not the case that everyone experiences a sense of continuing bonds with those who have died. And among those who do, this experience is not always comforting and healing. For instance, when a relationship with someone who has died was painful or deeply problematic, it may be hard to take comfort in memories or actively embrace the person's legacy. Ministers want to bring great sensitivity to this area of grief care. Ministers can also support people in finding balance in the area of continuing bonds. While one may draw comfort and meaning from a sense of ongoing connection to the deceased, one must still move into one's future with hope and trust in God's promises, including the promise that we will all be raised on the last day and enjoy eternal life (John 6:40). And while continuing bonds with deceased loved ones may be both powerful and healing, we must remember that the Christian's primary relationship is with the living Christ. The real and ongoing presence of Christ in our lives is the ultimate continuing bond.

The Balancing Act of Grief Care

The ministry of grief care poses particular challenges. While many feel drawn to this ministry as especially fulfilling at an essential level, it is often a delicate balancing act, both personally and professionally. I would like to suggest three efforts that might help ministers to maintain their balance as they offer grief care.

First, *ministers must be self-aware regarding their own history of loss.* Self-awareness is a critical cornerstone of all pastoral care and counseling. However, in grief care this self-awareness must pertain in an intentional way to one's own history of and current experience of loss. Bearing witness to and responding to the grief of others may affect or provoke ministers in powerful and some-times painful ways. For example, hearing others describe their regrets after a loss may stir up our regrets from the past. Accompanying others who feel abandoned or punished by God in their suffering may prompt our own questions about God's presence and role in suffering. These responses may be terribly painful and could adversely affect the care we offer another. For instance, we may neglect or minimize parts of another's struggle that are too painfully close to our own. Self-awareness regarding our own experi-ence of loss may help us in multiple ways as we offer grief care. It may help us to recognize and monitor our powerful responses to another's grief. It may help us to respond to others in free and nonreactive ways. It may also help us to recognize moments when we may not be the best person to care for another, given our particular experience of loss.

The second effort that might help ministers to maintain their balance as they offer grief care is *attending to self-care and particularly guarding against vicarious traumatization*. We are increasingly aware of the sometimes danger-ous stress of working with others in need and of how essential consistent self-care is.[8] In considering the experience of psychotherapists who work with trauma survivors, Lisa McCann and Laurie Anne Pearlman have described the phenomenon of "vicarious traumatization" (1990, 133). A terrible effect of trauma can be changes in basic cognitive schemas about what life is like and how the world works. For example, a trauma survivor may come to believe that the world is not safe or that others are not trust-worthy. Over time, clinicians who listen to the sometimes horrifying stories of trauma survivors may experience parallel changes in their own cogni-tive schemas about life; that is, they experience vicarious traumatization.

Clearly, ministers who work with survivors of terrible loss, some of it traumatic, may be at risk of vicarious traumatization. Vicarious traumati-zation benefits no one and may render a caregiver less responsive to those needing grief care. Therefore, it is essential to avoid it or minimize its effects as much as possible. McCann and Pearlman offer suggestions for clinicians at risk of vicarious traumatization; their suggestions are help-ful for ministers as well. For example, they describe the importance of having a peer group for regular support and processing of painful client material (with client permission). They also make recommendations that emphasize balance, such as "striving for balance between our personal

and professional lives" and "balancing a clinical caseload with other professional involvements such as research and teaching that can replenish
us" (1990, 146). Ministers, too, must seek such balance as essential for
self-care.

The third effort that might help ministers to maintain their balance
as they offer grief care is *encouraging and allowing the larger community of faith
to do its part in caring for those who grieve.* Sometimes ministers feel enormous
responsibility to care for those made vulnerable by loss and grief. This
sense of responsibility may blind us to the critical role that the faith community plays in caring for those who grieve. It is important to remember
that "pastoral work with mourners is the work of the congregation, not
just of certain professionals" (Mitchell & Anderson 1983, 11).[9] Some congregations offer lay pastoral caregiving programs that might be helpful to
those in grief.[10] Even without such programs, however, the community of
faith offers grief care through its supportive presence, its prayers for one
another, and its witness to God's fidelity and compassion. Understanding
that the faith community serves in these ways can help ministers to feel
more balanced. Grief care is the work of all the faithful; it is most defi-
nitely not all up to us.

The Mosaic of Grief

In eastern Turkey lie the remains of the ancient city of Zeugma, founded
in 300 B.C.E. by one of the generals of Alexander the Great. Zeugma,
strategically located along the Euphrates River, was a vital and prosper-
ous center of trade and culture as part of the Greek world and later the
Roman Empire. It appears that it was destroyed by fire in 250 C.E. and has
largely remained buried under many feet of sediment ever since. In recent
years, archaeologists and historians became fiercely interested in Zeugma
because, as part of an elaborate national engineering project, the Turkish
government planned to construct a dam that would flood the remains of
Zeugma. Racing against the clock to excavate parts of the area and rescue
what they could, archaeologists were stunned to unearth exquisite and
elaborate mosaics from the ancient Roman world, depicting important
scenes from literature and mythology in rich color and intricate detail.
These priceless and historic masterpieces were saved just in time. But,

sadly, archaeologists were not able to excavate all of Zeugma before it was flooded in 2000. They feel certain that other ancient mosaic masterpieces now lie under the floodwaters of the Euphrates.[11]

The experience of grief is particular, intricate, and nuanced. When we are not aware of the many dimensions of grief, another's grief experience may be utterly lost to us, like the mosaics of Zeugma now hidden beneath the Euphrates. Fortunately, the contemporary grief field offers us great riches to deepen our understanding of the grief experience and thereby to inform our care of others. When we understand such aspects as chronic sorrow, grief born of injustice, the trajectories of grief, and continuing bonds with the deceased, we are less likely to disenfranchise another's grief. We will see another's mosaic of grief in more color and detail. And this will help us to offer sensitive and appropriate care. But we must remember that grief care is challenging and requires that we be self-aware regarding our own experience of loss, attend to self-care while avoiding or minimizing vicarious traumatization, and celebrate the role of the faith community in caring for those who grieve. All of these efforts will help to sustain us as we pursue this challenging but tremendously important work.

2

The History of Grief Theory

IN SIGNIFICANT WAYS, the contemporary work on grief presented in this book represents a real break from the past. This chapter helps to situate the new theory against its historical backdrop. In this chapter, we will visit some important markers in the history of thought about grief. We will hear varied voices on grief from antiquity to the present day. We will also review important pillars of grief theory, from its long-standing psychoanalytic home to the familiar stage-theory paradigm. Many aspects of traditional grief theory have come under fire in recent years, and this chapter synthesizes three contemporary critiques of the traditional grief field: first, a critique of the standard psychoanalytic model of grieving; second, a critique of stage-theory models of grieving; and third, a cultural critique of some traditional ways of understanding grief. We conclude with further thoughts on the mosaic of grief.

Early Perspectives on Grief

As long as people have been thinking and writing, it seems, they have been sharing their reflections on grief. In antiquity, philosophers and poets mused about different dimensions of grief.[1] For example, the great Greek dramatist Sophocles (c. 496–406 B.C.E.) spoke of the power of grief to unsettle when he wrote, "Grief teaches the steadiest minds to waver." His countryman Euripides (c. 484–406 B.C.E.) expressed something of the need for companionship in grieving when he wrote, "I loathe a friend whose gratitude grows old, / a friend who takes his friend's prosperity / but will not voyage with him in his grief." Several centuries later, the Roman poet Ovid (43 B.C.E.–17 C.E.) cautioned about the dangers of unexpressed grief in these words: "A grief that is checked simply chokes us, seething and boiling within us, / And is forced in its straitened location to multiply all of its strength." We might even see humor—whether intended or not—in the words of the Roman philosopher and statesman Cicero (106–43 B.C.E.): "It is folly to tear one's hair in sorrow, as if grief could be assuaged by baldness."

Through the centuries, literary writers have continued to reflect on these themes, perhaps none more eloquently than William Shakespeare. One can hear shades of Ovid's words in the following line from *Macbeth*: "Give sorrow words: the grief that does not speak / Whispers the o'er-fraught heart and bids it break" (IV, iii). And one hears the pain of silent grief in this line from *King Richard II*: "My grief lies all within / And these external manners of laments / Are merely shadows to the unseen grief / That swells with silence in the tortured soul" (IV, i). Also, the nineteenth-century poet Emily Dickinson described a comparative dimension of her grief in this moving line: "I measure every grief I meet / With analytic eyes; / I wonder if it weighs like mine, / Or has an easier size."[2]

Of course, Scripture is a timeless source of insight and consolation about the experience of grief. Many characters in Scripture have spoken poignantly about their grief. For example, Job expressed his deep pain in these words: "My eye has grown dim from grief, and all my members are like a shadow" (Job 17:7). Likewise, the prophet Jeremiah expressed his deep pain: "My joy is gone, grief is upon me, my heart is sick" (Jer. 8:18). Multiple psalms express the raw pain of grief. For example, in Psalm 6:7 we hear: "My eyes waste away because of grief; they grow weak because of all my foes." The psalmist pleads with God in Psalm 31:9: "Be gracious to me, O LORD, for I am in distress; my eye wastes away from grief, my soul and body also." In Psalm 10:14, we see something of the psalmist's hope and trust that God responds to those in grief: "But you do see! Indeed you note trouble and grief, that you may take it into your hands; the helpless commit themselves to you; you have been the helper of the orphan."

In the New Testament, we hear the very poignant and human words of Jesus in the garden of Gethsemane as he contemplated the suffering and pain that lay before him: "And he said to them, 'I am deeply grieved, even to death; remain here, and keep awake'" (Mark 14:34). We know the disciples did not keep awake in the garden. Fascinatingly, Luke the Evangelist seems to offer insight into this behavior of the disciples when he writes, "When he got up from prayer, he came to the disciples and found them sleeping because of grief" (Luke 22:45). Luke seems to suggest that, rather than being unsympathetic or just plain sleepy, the disciples may have been overwhelmed with their own grief, perhaps in response to the sobering and solemn words of Jesus in the prior days. Finally, Paul implores the Thessalonians not to lose hope in their grief: "But we do not want you to be uninformed, brothers and sisters, about those who have died, so that you may not grieve as others do who have no hope" (1 Thess. 4:13).

Thus, it seems clear that the experience of grief and reflections on this experience have long been part and parcel of the human and Judeo-Christian stories. However, how people have understood and explained grief has varied greatly across time. Some have written of grief as a natural and inevitable human response to loss. For example, in *The Expression of the Emotions in Man and Animals* (1872), Charles Darwin proposes that many animal species, including human beings, emit a distinctive cry of sorrow when they experience separation from other significant creatures. He postulates that the "grief muscles" produce this seemingly instinctive cry following loss (Parkes 2001, 26). Historically, grief has often been described as problematic, difficult, even dangerous. Some have written of grief as a disruptive and potentially detrimental process that may lead to physical and mental illness. British psychiatrist Colin Murray Parkes describes some of the earliest extant writings that link loss with mental or physical maladies:

> Thus Robert Burton, in *The Anatomy of Melancholie* (1621), refers to grief or sorrow as "The epitome, symptome and chief cause" of melancholia or, as it would be termed today, clinical depression. In the same century

we find "griefe" acceptable as a cause of death in Heberden's *Bills of Mortality of the City of London* for 1657. The idea that grief itself can take a pathological form was current by 1703 when Vogther, in *Altdorf*, published a thesis, "*De Morbis Moerentium*," in which he prescribed a variety of medications for pathological grief. The dangers of bereavement were also emphasised by Benjamin Rush, one of the signatories of the American Declaration of Independence, who advised bereaved people to avoid reminders of their loss and to take "liberal doses of opium" (1835). He too saw grief as a potential cause of death and described post-mortem findings in people who had died of rupture of the auricles and ventricles of the heart following bereavement, literally dying from a "broken heart." (ibid.)

Much of this variation in understanding the experience of grief disappeared in the West in the twentieth century with the rise of psychoanalysis and its definitive description of grief.

Psychoanalytic Understanding of Grief

Without a doubt, the field of psychoanalysis has profoundly influenced how many people understand grief today, and so we must begin with the work of Sigmund Freud. Although he did not write extensively on the topic of mourning (the traditional psychoanalytic term for grief), Freud's work shaped psychoanalytic thought regarding the experience and process of grief, and his work continues to inform the standard psychoanalytic approach to and treatment of grief (Hagman 2001). In *Mourning and Melancholia* (1957 [1917]), Freud proposes both differences and similarities between mourning and melancholia (what we would today call depression). According to Freud, the "work of mourning" (245) involves one universal project. The person in mourning must withdraw libido (energy) from the object that has been lost (i.e., *decathexis*) in order to redirect it toward another, available object. Here are Freud's own words on the topic:

> In what, now, does the work which mourning performs consist? ... Reality-testing has shown that the loved object no longer exists, and it proceeds to demand that all libido shall be withdrawn from its attachments to that object. This demand arouses understandable opposition—it is a

matter of general observation that people never willingly abandon a libidinal position, not even, indeed, when a substitute is already beckoning to them. This opposition can be so intense that a turning away from reality takes place and a clinging to the object through the medium of a hallucinatory wishful psychosis. Normally, respect for reality gains the day. Nevertheless its orders cannot be obeyed at once. They are carried out bit by bit, at great expense of time and cathectic energy, and in the meantime the existence of the lost object is psychically prolonged. Each single one of the memories and expectations in which the libido is bound to the object is brought up and hypercathected, and detachment of the libido is accomplished in respect of it. . . . The fact is. . . that when the work of mourning is completed the ego becomes free and uninhibited again. (1957 [1917], 244–45)

In some cases, particularly following the death of someone whom one has loved ambivalently, one may experience melancholia rather than normal mourning. In such cases, the negative feelings that one has toward the deceased person are internalized and become part of the survivor's own sense of self. Thus, the survivor will experience a loss of self-esteem, depression, and self-blame. In the Freudian formulation, this significant blow to one's sense of self is a hallmark of melancholia, rather than normal mourning, and this basic distinction between mourning and melancholia is still largely accepted today (Kaplan, Sadock, & Grebb 1994). Thus, with Freud's ideas, the "standard psychoanalytic model of mourning" (Hagman 2001, 14) began to take shape, and it continued to develop in the succeeding decades.

Critique of the Standard Psychoanalytic Model of Mourning

Grief theorists and clinicians who have been trained psychoanalytically, and many who have not, often continue to draw on the standard psychoanalytic model to inform their work. In addition, many aspects of the standard model have deeply penetrated cultural beliefs and expectations about grief at large, including those of ministers. Certain foundational aspects of the standard model have come under scrutiny of late. George Hagman (2001) offers a helpful synthesis of various aspects of the standard model as well as the critique of the model being levied by some contemporary psychoanalytic writers.[3] He also describes features of the "new psychoanalytic model of mourning" (24) now emerging. I will present some of Hagman's work in eight primary points and offer some commentary. As we consider key features of the standard model, let's reflect on the degree to which the suppositions of the standard model may have shaped our own understanding of grief.

Standard Model: A Norm for Mourning

The standard psychoanalytic model suggests that there is a normal way to mourn. It is not interested in how a person's experience of loss may be particular. That is, once a loss has occurred, the road ahead is laid out fairly clearly, regardless of the individual, familial, societal, cultural, religious, and contextual factors that may shape one's experience of the loss and consequent grief.

This prescription of a normal and universal path through grief has sometimes functioned as an unhelpful or even destructive template for grieving people who, on top of everything else with which they are coping, have to worry about whether they are grieving normally. I have heard this concern raised by grieving people who sometimes say things such as, "I'm not sure I'm grieving correctly," or "Am I doing this right?" In contrast, the emerging psychoanalytic perspective acknowledges and affirms the innumerable and varied factors that may shape one's response to loss. It acknowledges that each person will experience and respond to loss in his or her own way.

Standard Model: A Prescribed Time for Mourning

The standard model maintains that the process of normal mourning is "time limited" and ends in a complete resolution of the loss (Hagman 2001, 19). From this perspective, grief does not go on and on. There is an end point when one is done grieving, and nothing residual remains.

This assumption may lead some people to feel they are grieving poorly or unsuccessfully if they do not come to a clear and full end point to grief. Others may reinforce this belief. For example, I once invited an acquaintance to speak in a grief and loss course that I teach to ministry students. Barbara's daughter, Heather, had died nine or ten years prior, in her junior year of high school. From my perspective, Barbara had coped remarkably well with her loss over time, going on with her life, doing meaningful work, sustaining rich relationships with her family and friends. It was also clear that she continued to feel the great loss of Heather and sought ways to maintain a sense of connection with her. For instance, she found ways—such as through memory books and photo albums—to let her grandchildren know about the aunt they would never meet.

What was both surprising and striking to me about Barbara's presence in my class was the response of a few students. They expressed great concern and frustration that Barbara seemed "stuck" in her grief. Why was she still talking about her daughter ten years after her death? Why hadn't she let go completely and moved on? I don't think these comments and frustrations reflected any lack of compassion on their part. Rather, I think they had somehow absorbed from the culture the cherished assumption that grief is a temporary state and that a definitive end point does exist.

I remember another situation involving a young mother whose newborn baby died within days of her birth. The mother was devastated and sought support from a clergyperson, who was an acquaintance of mine. This clergyperson was initially very sympathetic and kind to the mother. After a couple of months, though, she said to me with exasperation, "Why isn't she over this already? She's got to move on!" Clearly, she was ready for the mother to have reached the end of her grief.

In contrast to this aspect of the standard model, the emerging psychoanalytic perspective suggests that "mourning is not something that can be finished" (Gaines 1997, 568). For many people, there may never be a definitive "end point" to their grief. Rather, people learn to live with their grief. The acuity and pain of the grief tend to subside over time. However, people may reexperience pain, sadness, longing, or other feelings when they recall their lost loved one. Grief becomes a new character in one's life narrative, perhaps largely receding into the wings over time but never fully vacating the stage and capable of making an entrance at particular moments throughout one's life. I remember my mother once recalling the day her father had died, probably thirty years earlier. She was ironing a dress to wear to the hospital so that her father would not be alone when she got the call that he had just died. She teared up as she shared this story, although she hastened to reassure me, "I'm okay! I don't know why I'm crying!" Even after thirty years, a sad memory had prompted a moment of grief.

Standard Model: A Return to Normal

The standard model suggests that mourning serves to restore a person to preloss status or functioning, rather than to transform a person in some way. That is, if one grieves successfully (i.e., normally), one will basically "get back to normal" in a matter of time. And "normal" means one's way of being before the death or major loss. This perspective seems to view grief as a temporary blip on the screen of one's life, not a potential passage to a new or changed way of being.

In contrast, the emerging perspective suggests that a significant loss may well change us or even transform us in a fundamental and ongoing way (Pollock 1989), and thus there is no going back to what life was like before the loss. We may resume our jobs, schedules, and habits, but we are changed by the loss in ways that we may not understand for a long time. Some grieving people feel that even the suggestion that they could get back to "normal" after their loss is offensive and minimizes the depth and strength of their connection to the deceased. Some people describe feeling that a "new normal" emerges after a major loss, although it can take a long time for this new normal to take shape. For some people, the new normal is a grim, taxing reality, at least for a time. A widowed woman expressed to me something about her painful new normal: "I am no less sad now than I was when my husband died ten months ago, but I am more accustomed to the sadness. I have learned to live with it. I have adjusted in the same way you would eventually adjust to becoming blind."

While finding the new normal can be wrenchingly painful, there may be graced aspects of the process as well. Gerald Caplan (1964), the father of crisis theory in the United States, understood a crisis as a "turning point" that could potentially lead to personal growth. Many researchers have discovered that a crisis such as a significant death can lead to some helpful or positive growth, such as enhancement of coping skills, of one's relationships with others, and of one's sense of self.[4] Let me hasten to add that *this is not the same as saying that one is glad the loss has occurred.* But given that a loss has occurred, many people describe feeling that they have grown in positive ways from their *struggle* with the loss (Calhoun & Tedeschi 2001). The following quotes, shared with me by grieving people, describe some positive growth following painful loss:

- ◆ "I know the death brought my dad and I [sic] closer—there were many hugs going around and I think I learned a new way to express my love for my dad. The death pulled my family together."

- ◆ "I have a growing appreciation for beauty. I find greater satisfaction in the immediate, especially in regard to relationships. I'm freer to appreciate the simple interactions with loved ones."

- ◆ "My brother's death helps me to realize that life is short and precious and that I must live every day to the fullest. . . . I value life so much now. I want to make the most of every moment. My family and friends are my number-one priority—nothing is more important to me now."

- ◆ "I've gone back to writing fiction and also I've picked up knitting, which I thought is good therapy, but it's interesting how you reach a point in the grief where you're so low and you're so broken, but you're also the most open to anything, new thoughts, new things to do, and maybe that's the little blessing that you can hang on to. What have you got to lose, and you're interested because you're tired of being so low."

Thus, amid the sadness and struggle, there may be graced dimensions on the road to the new normal. People may be changed in life-giving ways by and through their loss.

Standard Model: The End of Connection

According to the standard model, the purpose of mourning is to withdraw all psychic energy (i.e., to decathect) from the lost loved one in order to be able to reinvest it in new relationships. Any sense that one continues to feel an attachment to the deceased loved one may be evidence of pathology. When a person dies, he or she is dead and gone.

So pervasive and insistent has been this understanding of grief that some people have considered themselves crazy for feeling that they still maintain a connection in more than memory with the deceased other. Or at least they may have hesitated to disclose this sense of connection. For instance, Joan and Erik Erikson and colleague Helen Kivnick (1986), writing about the final developmental stage of life, report that several octogenarians whom they interviewed had experienced moments of a quite powerful connection with their deceased spouses. Most of them did not proffer this information, but when asked whether they had had such experiences, they described them eagerly in vivid detail.

As we saw in the last chapter, important work in recent years has looked at the continuity of relationship with the deceased that many people describe.[5] Researchers Dennis Klass, Phyllis Silverman, and Steven Nickman (1996) introduced the term *continuing bonds* to describe this experience. Let me offer two examples of such continuing bonds. Elizabeth Edwards, an attorney and the wife of former vice-presidential candidate John Edwards from North Carolina, has written about the tragic death of their oldest child, Wade, who was killed in an automobile accident when he was sixteen. In *Saving Graces* (2006), Edwards writes that there is no question for her that she is still in relationship with her son; for instance, she writes of her various efforts to "parent the memory of Wade" (98).

Above I mentioned Barbara, whose daughter, Heather, died in high school. As Heather was undergoing cancer treatments, neighbors and other members of her community placed rainbow-colored ribbons all around town because Heather loved rainbows. Before she died, Heather told her family, "Whenever you see a rainbow, I'll be with you." Today, many years after Heather's death, unexpected rainbow sightings are important and precious reminders to this family of Heather's ongoing presence in their lives.

Standard Model: No Focus on Meaning

The standard model, so focused on the goal and process of *decathexis*, is not particularly interested in the meaning or meanings that a significant loss may carry for the survivor.

Meaning is an interesting and sometimes confusing concept. It is a common word, but not always used with clarity or precision. What do we *mean* by words such as *meaning* and *meaningful*? This is an important point for us because the concept of *meaning* has begun to take center stage in much grief research and care. Chapter 4 is dedicated to an exploration of what is meant by *meaning* in the context of grief and loss. For now, we can say that *meaning* may suggest, in part, the sense we make of a loss, how we fit the loss into our overarching worldview and system of beliefs, how we form coherence in our life narrative given the loss. And it is in this context that the standard model comes under criticism. The area of meaning-seeking and meaning-finding following loss is not an aspect taken up by the standard model. In contrast, according to Hagman, the emerging psychoanalytic theory of mourning understands mourning as "a crisis of meaning" (2001, 22). In struggling with a significant death, people may need to seek meaning in, of, and after the loss.

Standard Model: An Individual Experience

The standard model suggests that mourning is largely an individual, intrapsychic experience. That is, grief is a private affair, to be conducted by an individual within his or her own psyche. It is not a relational or social phenomenon; it does not involve other people in an essential way.

We probably are familiar with how this prescription is often enacted. For instance, in some families or cultures, people are expected to grieve in private, when no one is around. In the presence of others, they ought to keep a stiff upper lip, especially around children (e.g., "You must be strong for the children"). As a college campus minister, I used to run grief support groups for anyone who had experienced a death. Student after student, when asked if they were able to talk with their friends about their loss, replied that they tended to keep everything to themselves because they didn't want to "be a wet blanket" or "ruin everyone's fun." They had learned well that grief ought to be individual and private.

A contemporary critique is that this aspect of the standard model denies or ignores social and relational features of grief. In contrast, the emerging psychoanalytic model of mourning understands that grief is not a private event but rather an "intersubjective process" (Hagman

2001, 25). The relational dimensions of grief can be understood in multiple ways. For instance, Gerald Caplan emphasized the importance of relationships as one copes with and potentially grows through a crisis. Caplan was instrumental in expanding conceptions of loss to events other than death. He studied extensively the experiences of women who had had very premature babies. He concluded that those women who had received help in acknowledging and dealing with the severity of the event often had better psychological outcomes.

> Every crisis presents both an opportunity for psychological growth and the danger of psychological deterioration. It is a way station on a path leading away from or toward mental disorder. The outcome of the crisis depends on the resolution of a complex of conflicting forces during the period of the disequilibrium. Some of the forces originate inside the individual and relate to his personality structure and past biopsychosocial experience. Some of the forces originate in his current environment, particularly changes in the intensity of the hazardous circumstances and the help or hindrance of other people, his family and friends, and those formal and informal care-giving persons to whom he may turn. . . . Crisis therefore presents care-giving persons with a remarkable opportunity to deploy their efforts to maximum advantage in influencing the mental health of others. (Caplan 1964, 53–54)

Another relational aspect of grief is that grief may change people. Who one is in relationships will likely be different after a major loss, and the relationships must find a way to accommodate these changes. The relational dimensions of grief will be explored in depth in chapter 6.

Standard Model: Affective Dimension

According to the standard model, grief *affect* is a normal and spontaneous part of the experience of mourning and is suppressed only at the risk of psychopathology. *Affect* is another word for the numerous emotions humans can experience. Often we expect people who have suffered a major loss to demonstrate affect, at least initially; perhaps most commonly, we expect people to be sad. When they don't seem sad, we might supply judgment. For instance, we may think, "She hasn't shed a tear. She's really in denial," or "He doesn't even seem that upset. I wonder if he really cared after all." The judgment embedded in such comments is clear: the expression of affect is an expected part of grief.

The emerging psychoanalytic perspective, which considers the uniqueness of each person's grief, might lead us to question this premise. Why would we expect and even prescribe the expression of affect as part of every grief experience? Wouldn't it make sense that people, in all their great variety, would experience and express affect to considerably greater or lesser degrees? Of course, an absence of affect during grief may be cause for concern. For instance, it may indicate that a person has not been able to absorb the reality of the loss. In general, though, the realm of affect in grief is likely marked by great complexity and particularity.

Standard Model: Painful Emotions

The standard model of grief maintains that when one experiences grief affect, it will be painful; normal mourning will not encompass a variety of affect, including, for example, pleasure or humor. In fact, experiencing and/or expressing pleasure or humor or other positive emotions would be considered problematic or even pathological. A very popular television comedy show from the 1970s makes this point. On *The Mary Tyler Moore Show*, the beloved TV character Chuckles the Clown has died, squished by an elephant while he was dressed like a peanut. In the face of such a bizarre death, many of the characters on the show make jokes. Mary, the main character, scolds them for their inappropriate humor and reminds them of what a terrible tragedy this is. When they get to the memorial service and hear tributes to Chuckles, the other characters are solemn and quiet. Mary, however, begins to laugh and cannot stop.

In contrast, the emerging psychoanalytic perspective suggests that a range of emotions—including "positive affects such as joy and pride" (Hagman 2001, 27)—may be part of the grief experience. People may feel great gratitude in reflecting on life with the deceased. They may feel joy as they recall wonderful, graced moments with the other. They may feel pleasure and calm as they think of the peaceful death. They may feel relief that the suffering of their loved one or the strain of constant caregiving is over. They may laugh as they recall the deceased's great storytelling personality or odd, comical moments during the final days.

For instance, my husband and his brother enjoyed a moment of poignant humor in the midst of their sadness when their father died. Their father was a proper, dignified man who always dressed carefully and sometimes scolded his sons in their youth for sloppy attire. When his sons discovered that he would not be buried with shoes on, they laughed affectionately at this little irony. The contemporary perspective suggests that this range of emotions, including positive and pleasurable emotions, may well be part of healthy grieving and is not to be discouraged or condemned.

Further Dimensions of Traditional Grief Theory

While Freud's work and the psychoanalytic thought flowing from it have profoundly shaped traditional understandings of grief, there are other key theorists and theories whose contributions to the field have been seminal. We will now take a brief look at these important theorists and theories.

Erich Lindemann

On November 28, 1942, a devastating fire broke out in the Cocoanut Grove nightclub in Boston, Massachusetts, killing 492 people and injuring many others. This horrendous tragedy marked a major turning point in several areas. First, it prompted changes in fire-safety laws across the United States. Second, it ushered in new developments in the medical treatment of victims of fire and smoke inhalation. Third, this horrific event crystallized a new understanding of the grief experience, due largely to the work of Erich Lindemann, who, at the time of the fire, was a psychiatrist at Massachusetts General Hospital in Boston. He worked with many of the survivors of the fire, as well as their family members. In 1944, Lindemann published his careful observations of some of these people, along with other groups of bereaved people, and he described the common presentation and symptomatology of those experiencing acute grief:

> Common to all is the following syndrome: sensations of somatic distress occurring in waves lasting from twenty minutes to an hour at a time, a feeling of tightness in the throat, choking with shortness of breath, need

for sighing, and an empty feeling in the abdomen, lack of muscular power, and an intense subjective distress described as tension or mental pain. (1944, 141)

Lindemann described five common features that seemed to mark the grief of these people: "(1) somatic distress, (2) preoccupation with the image of the deceased, (3) guilt, (4) hostile reactions, and (5) loss of patterns of conduct" (ibid., 142). He suggested that these common features were the hallmarks of a normal grief response.[6] Lindemann's work was a defining moment in the still-new field of grief research, and his descriptions of his observations became for many the template for "normal" grief.

John Bowlby and Attachment Theory

One of the most important cornerstones of grief theory in the twentieth century and still today is attachment theory, first formulated for psychiatry by British psychiatrist John Bowlby. The next chapter is focused specifically on attachment theory and attachment to God as critical contemporary lenses for considering the experience of grief, and therefore we will not review attachment theory here. Suffice it to say, though, that the work of John Bowlby and his colleagues has been and remains indispensable for many grief theorists and clinicians.

Stage Theory

If we were to ask the average person on the street about how normal dying and/or grieving is supposed to go, it is quite possible that we would hear something about stages. "Stage theory" of dying and of grief has become deeply embedded in our culture. Let's take a look at stage theory and at the origins of these ideas.

The major theories of grief that we have surveyed suggest that there are tasks, processes, or stages that grieving persons will experience and in a largely invariant sequence. Freud (1957 [1917]) used the metaphor of the "work of mourning" to describe the universal project of those who grieve: gradually to withdraw libido from the deceased person in order to be able to invest this energy in a new relationship. Lindemann extended this theoretical line when he described the process of "grief work," "namely, emancipation from the bondage to the deceased, readjustment to the environment in which the deceased is missing, and the formation of new relationships" (1944, 143). In attachment theory, Bowlby, in collaboration with Parkes (Bowlby & Parkes 1970), proposed four biologically based "phases of grief": "(a) numbness, (b) yearning and searching, (c) disorganization and despair, and (d) reorganization" (Parkes 2001, 29–30).

In the area of death and dying, psychiatrist Elisabeth Kübler-Ross (1969) has been profoundly influential. Drawing on her work with dying hospital patients, she proposed that those facing their own impending death will typically experience five stages. In the first stage, dying patients will experience shock at the news of their impending death and may then *deny* this reality. In the second stage, patients experience *anger* at the reality that they are dying. This anger may be directed toward family, friends, hospital personnel, God, or themselves. In the third stage, that of *bargaining*, patients may attempt to strike a deal with hospital personnel, others, or God; for example, in exchange for recovery and continued life, the patients will behave in some exemplary way or will fulfill some promise. In the fourth stage, patients will experience symptoms of *depression* as they come to understand the reality of their impending death and the effects of this reality on their current situation. In the fifth stage, patients come to *accept* the reality of their impending death.

It is no exaggeration to say that Kübler-Ross's stage paradigm of dying has taken on a life of its own and has become deeply embedded not only in the field of thanatology but in culture more broadly. Two humorous examples illustrate this embeddedness. In one episode of the long-running cartoon series *The Simpsons*, the buffoonish Homer Simpson thinks he has eaten poisonous fish and has been told that he will therefore die within twenty-four hours. Upon hearing this death sentence, he immediately embarks on the five stages of dying in rapid succession, reaching "acceptance" within a matter of seconds.

Here is another example. In a recent issue of a travel magazine, an advertisement for a tropical island features a beautiful golf course. Various holes of the golf course are labeled with the stages of dying. Then, in a creative addition, one of the last holes is labeled "love." I shared this ad with students in my grief and loss course and admitted that I didn't really understand why the stages of dying were being applied to a golf course, followed by the stage of "love." One of my students replied, "You're obviously not a golfer." (Apparently, some golfers experience great highs and lows; they might feel the game is killing them, and then, with one good shot, they are in love with it all over again.) These silly examples demonstrate just how widespread and embedded in our culture are ideas about the stages of dying.

Critique of Stage Theory

While these stages have been highly formative in studies of dying, many have also applied these precise stages to the experience of grieving. To do so presumes that the experience of dying and the experience of grieving a death are parallel or even identical processes. Professor David Switzer has labeled this conflation both "distorting and misleading" (1990, 473). This unquestioning embrace of "stage theory" of grieving has come under scrutiny, especially since scientific studies have not yielded clear evidence of such stages among those in grief (Neimeyer 2001c). Some contemporary grief theorists have critiqued the concept of stages of grieving as inaccurate, seriously limited, and unhelpful.[7] In particular, stage theory faces challenges for its prescriptive, rather than descriptive, emphasis. Proposals of stages or phases of grieving suggest an invariant universality of human experience that neglects individual, familial, religious, societal, cultural, and contextual factors. The stages are presumed to capture normal or healthy experience, and anyone whose experience does not follow the stages precisely or completely risks being labeled unhealthy, avoidant, abnormal, or otherwise pathological.

Here is a powerful example of such unhelpful labeling. A colleague once described a disturbing experience he had while working as a hospital chaplain. After some heartfelt conversations, a dying patient described feeling at peace and ready to die. When the chaplain shared this with the patient's physician, the physician grew agitated and exclaimed, "She is not ready to die. She is only at stage three!" This illustrates the potential danger of slavish adherence to "stage theory"—it can lead to the point where one cannot or will not take in another's actual experience.

Cultural Critique of Traditional Grief Theory

A final and very important contemporary critique of traditional grief theory is that it has been steeped in cultural bias and/or cultural neglect. As
Parkes notes, "Most of the early studies of the psychology of bereavement
were conducted by psychiatrists on samples of White, Christian widows.
This has resulted in a culturally biased view of 'normal grief'" (2001,
34). Paul Rosenblatt has done some of the best contemporary work on
grief and culture, and he makes a similar point: "Much of what is written about grieving comes from the perceptions, writing, and editing of
educated Americans and Europeans" (2001, 288). Rosenblatt himself has
developed a social constructionist view of grief. This perspective asserts
that much of what people understand about grief and how they express
grief is socially constructed; that is, the society and/or culture in which
we live shapes our thoughts, feelings, and behaviors when we are grieving. This social shaping accounts for some of the tremendous variation in
grief expression across cultures. In a study of cultures by Rosenblatt, for
example:

> There were cultures in which anger and aggression were a central part
> of grief and cultures in which they were seemingly never expressed in
> grief, cultures in which self-mutilation was a part of grief and cultures
> in which it was not. There were cultures in which grief for a close family
> member would often go on for years and cultures in which grief, at least
> on the surface, typically disappeared quickly. (ibid., 289)

There may also be great variation in grieving norms and practices within
a particular culture. For example, an international student once told me
that, in her culture, only women should publicly grieve. If a man displays
his grief, he is pejoratively described as a "woman."

While asserting that little about grief appears to be universal, Rosenblatt does acknowledge that one thing seems to be true in all cultures
which he has studied, and that is that death is difficult. How this difficulty
is experienced and expressed—or not—varies tremendously, however,
both across and within cultures. "The difficulty was expressed through
tears, anger, personal disorganization, lamentation, depressed affect, or
difficulty engaging in some or all of what before the death would be normal activities" (ibid., 288). While proposing this one potentially common

feature of grief, Rosenblatt also asserts that whatever we think we might know for certain about grief—even the idea that death is difficult for all—ought to be considered "a temporarily solid base" (ibid., 287). As we learn more substantive, nuanced, and respectful means of studying grief across cultures, this base will no doubt take new shape.

In light of this important cultural critique, I want to acknowledge that this book also reflects some cultural limitations. The research and theory I share may or may not be applicable to people across cultures or even to all people within a culture, and so we must be careful not to draw any sweeping conclusions. Although this book offers some of the most contemporary understandings of grief, this may still be, at best, a "temporarily solid base" for understanding grief. We need to bring cultural curiosity to our ministry with others in order to understand their grief in more of its detail and vibrancy.

The Mosaic of Grief

Having reviewed these historical pillars of the grief field as well as some contemporary critiques, I hope we can now see ways in which the traditional grief field has seriously limited what we can understand and even see of another's grief experience. Emphasizing prescriptive aspects such as "normal" grief and "stages" of grief, the traditional grief field has promulgated a rather narrow and fixed understanding of grief. And this narrow and fixed understanding has sometimes left grieving people feeling alone, misunderstood, or even judged.

In the chapters that follow, we will explore in depth some key aspects of the contemporary grief field, integrated with important religious, theological, and pastoral perspectives. While traditional grief theory can often seem to encourage "paint-by-number" results, the contemporary field allows us—invites us—to understand each person's grief experience as a particular mosaic, fashioned out of innumerable and varied aspects of one's life, such as one's history of losses, one's relationships, one's ways of making meaning, one's experience of the Divine, one's religious resources, one's sense of community, one's culture, and so on. Each grief mosaic is unique, nuanced, and intricate. The aim of the chapters that follow is to give us eyes to see these works of art.

3

Attachment
Theory and
Attachment
to God

LIFE IS LIVED in relationships. When we think of all the possible relationships people may have, we can create an extensive list. We may have relationships with spouses, partners, parents, grandparents, siblings, children, grandchildren, and extended family. We may have relationships with close friends, acquaintances, classmates, colleagues, neighbors. We may have relationships with members of church communities, sports teams, civic associations, and service organizations. Each relationship plays a role in our lives, and each might shape in some way how we experience grief. One category of relationships plays a particularly substantial role in our experience of grief. These are called *attachment relationships*.

Attachment theory has long been a cornerstone of grief theory, and it continues to be a critical dimension of the contemporary secular grief world. In fact, an international survey of seventy-seven leading specialists in bereavement revealed that attachment theory and a psychodynamic perspective were their preferred perspectives for understanding grief (Middleton, Moylan, Raphael, Burnett & Martinek 1993). Attachment theory is also a critical lens for considering pastoral responses following loss (Dean 1988). Although attachment theory certainly cannot explain all the nuanced dimensions of one's response to loss, it does seem to carry us right to the heart of the grief experience.

Fascinatingly, despite decades of research and writing on human attachments, attachment theorists have paid scant attention to people's attachments, or relationships, to God. The area of attachment to God is still a largely unexplored frontier, although we are beginning to see that attachment to God may be a highly significant factor in one's experience of grief (Kelley 2003, 2009). We must understand not only how one's attachment to others may play a critical role in one's experience of grief but also how one's attachment to God might shape one's experience of grief, and perhaps profoundly so.

Case Vignette

The case vignette that follows and those in subsequent chapters are composite cases loosely drawn from my research and from my work in pastoral counseling and grief care. Any identifying information has been substantially altered to protect anonymity. As you read each case, I invite you to imagine that you have the opportunity to minister to the central character. I invite you to take note of your responses, feelings, questions, and concerns as you imagine this ministry. At the end of each chapter, I will provide some questions for further reflection.

> Corinne is an attorney in her late twenties whose mother, Theresa, died two years ago. Corinne is an only child and was born when Theresa was just seventeen. Corinne's birth father did not want to marry Theresa and moved away soon after finding out about the pregnancy. Corinne has only met her birth father twice and does not know where he currently lives. For the first eight years of Corinne's life, she and Theresa lived with Theresa's older sister, Ann, and Ann's husband. Corinne felt that she and her mother were more like siblings than mother and daughter. As Corinne was growing up, her mother would complain about her strict older sister, and Corinne would "cover" for her mother when she stayed out late at night. Theresa was generally a "fun" mother, but she was often impatient with Corinne and did not like how the demands of

motherhood interfered with her life. She left much of the day-to-day care of Corinne to her sister and brother-in-law. Corinne's aunt was a kind and gentle woman, but she was easily dominated by her husband. She would not defend Corinne when her husband was angry with the girl. Corinne adored her uncle but was also scared of him. He sometimes doted on Corinne and told her that she was very special. He was also strict and sometimes punished Corinne in harsh ways. He made it his mission to teach Corinne to take care of herself and reminded her regularly that most men could not be trusted. He died when Corinne was fourteen, and Corinne was devastated.

Growing up, Corinne went to church every weekend with her aunt. Corinne liked the people at church, and she liked to sing the hymns. Sometimes, though, she was confused about God. The hymns they sang were about God's love. However, the pastor talked a lot about sin, people's failings, and God's judgment. God seemed to be unpredictable, and Corinne was sometimes afraid of being sent to hell. She wasn't sure what it would take to keep God happy for her whole life. Corinne's mother and aunt taught her prayers to say before bed, and Corinne prayed faithfully every night.

When Corinne was eight, her mother began seeing a new boyfriend, Walter. At first, the three of them spent time together, and Corinne thought she might finally have a father. Eventually, Walter realized that he did not like children and gave Theresa a choice: she could stay with Corinne or marry him. Theresa chose Walter, and they moved several towns away. Theresa explained to Corinne that Corinne would continue to live with her aunt, and they would talk on the phone every day and see each other every weekend. Corinne felt the bottom fall out of her world, but there was nothing she could do. Corinne lived for her daily phone calls and weekly visits with her mother. She threw herself into school and was an excellent student. She had many good friends. Her teachers liked her and encouraged her to think about going to college and having a good career. Corinne was successful in college and, after working in business for a few years, was accepted at a prestigious law school in another state.

In Corinne's second year of law school, her mother was diagnosed with cancer. Corinne and her mother still talked every day, and Corinne experienced utter terror at the thought of losing her. When Theresa's condition worsened and she was told she had less than a year to live, Corinne took a leave of absence from school and went home. She began to pray incessantly that her mother would be healed, but this did not happen. Theresa's deterioration became more rapid. When the situation felt overwhelming to Corinne, the only thought with which she could comfort herself was that law school was waiting for her. In just three short months, Theresa died, and two weeks after that, Corinne was back at school. At first, she felt helpfully distracted by being back in classes, but that feeling did not last. Corinne felt overwhelmed with sorrow, anger, and profound loneliness. Over the next two years, the intensity of these feelings slowly abated, and Corinne successfully completed her law degree and found an excellent job.

Over these same two years, though, Corinne has felt deeply unsettled and adrift. She is not sure how to make sense of her mother's death, and she has troubling questions about the meaning of life. She does not know how to think about God's role in her mother's death. She remembers all the prayers she said for Theresa's healing, and she realizes that God didn't answer any of them. She has also experienced tremendous guilt for the times she looked forward to being back at school as her mother lay dying. She cannot stop wondering if her mother's death was in part punishment by God for all those selfish thoughts. Recently, Corinne has begun to attend services at her local church and now wishes to talk with her pastor about her experiences, feelings, and worries.

Attachment Theory

How can Corinne's pastor and her faith community help her in her grief and ongoing struggles? One important way to consider this question is through the lens of attachment theory. As you read the following overview of attachment theory, I invite you to make connections between the theory and Corinne's experiences both in childhood and in later years. In the next section, we will make some of these connections explicit. As you read, I invite you also to consider what your own experience of attachment relationships has been. It is often easier to incorporate an attachment perspective into our ministerial work when we have first understood attachment in ourselves.

Attachment theory was first formulated and developed for psychiatry by British psychoanalyst John Bowlby (1907–1990).[1] Bowlby's earliest work in attachment theory stemmed from his observational studies of young children separated from their families and placed in some sort of institution for a time. Bowlby and his colleague James Robertson identified specific behaviors that these children frequently demonstrated during such separations and proposed that these behaviors could be sorted into three phases: protest, despair, and detachment. During the first phase, that of protest, the children demonstrated significant separation distress. They screamed and cried, searched for the missing family member—usually the mother—and could not be soothed by other adults. During the second phase, that of despair, the children's behavior and demeanor suggested that they were losing hope for the return of their mothers. They became less active in protest and became more withdrawn. In the final phase, that of detachment, the children reengaged with the environment and demonstrated some openness to adult caregivers and to peers. When the children were reunited with their mothers, however, they did not demonstrate joy but rather seemed apathetic. In some cases, they turned away from their mothers and resisted reconnection for a time. Bowlby worked to understand the causes and purposes of such behaviors following separation. The groundbreaking result was his three-volume description of attachment theory, *Attachment and Loss* (1969, 1973, 1980).

Bowlby describes the behaviors demonstrated by children during separations from their families as attachment behaviors, and he proposes that attachment behaviors are instinctually intended to foster physical proximity to the caregiver, also known as the attachment figure. Consistent physical proximity to the attachment figure and appropriate responsiveness by the attachment figure to the needs of the infant foster a secure attachment in the infant. Secure attachments in infancy play a substantial role in one's capacity to form secure relationships later in life. Conversely, one who forms insecure attachments in infancy may also struggle with insecure relationships later in life. Bowlby maintains that attachment behavior is an instinctual and constitutive dimension of being human and endures throughout the life span. One never outgrows or develops beyond attachment behavior, but rather it persists, as Bowlby says, "from the cradle to the grave" (1979, 129). This claim has been supported empirically (Kaplan, Sadock, & Grebb 1994).

Based on laboratory observations of mothers and infants, Bowlby's colleague Mary Ainsworth denoted different patterns or styles of infant response to separations from their mothers. She labeled these styles "secure," "avoidant," and "resistant/ambivalent" (Ainsworth, Blehar, Waters, & Wall 1978).[2] Infants with a secure style of attachment have come, through experience, to expect their caregivers to be both accessible and responsive to their needs, and they thus feel more confident to explore and engage with the world. In contrast, infants with insecure attachments do not have the same confidence in the accessibility of their caregivers. Through experience, they have come to expect that caregivers are inconsistently available and that attachment behaviors are sometimes ignored or even rebuffed.

Among those classified as insecurely attached, infants may be designated as either "anxious-ambivalent" (analogous to Ainsworth's term "resistant/ambivalent") or "avoidant." Infants with an anxious-ambivalent attachment style chronically fear rejection by their attachment figures and become preoccupied with eliciting comfort and security from these attachment figures. Thus, their attachment system tends to be chronically activated. Infants with an avoidant attachment style have also come to anticipate rejection or lack of responsiveness from their attachment figures, and to suppress attachment feelings and behaviors as a defense against rejection (Fraley & Shaver 1999). As children and adults, they may demonstrate what Bowlby describes as "compulsive self-reliance" (1980, 171), maintaining emotional distance and limiting intimacy as a defensive, self-protective strategy (Feeney 1999).[3]

With Ainsworth's help, Bowlby refined the theory regarding the goal of attachment behaviors and the effects of separation. In the second volume of *Attachment and Loss* (1973), Bowlby posits that security in attachment derives from two things. Security in attachment is grounded, first, in a child's appraisal of an attachment figure as available and accessible and, second, in a child's appraisal of an attachment figure as responsive to the child's needs. Bowlby defines caregiver responsiveness as "willingness to act as comforter and protector" (1973, 201). Bowlby then proposes that the term *availability* is inclusive of both the accessibility and the responsiveness of the caregiver and thus could be used to name the goal of the attachment behavioral system.

The expectations that one has regarding caregiver availability (that is, accessibility and responsiveness) are functions of internal working models, which are "cognitive/affective schemas, or representations" (Bartholomew & Shaver 1998, 25) of both self and others that are formed as a result of one's actual experiences in attachment relationships. Internal working models, according to Bowlby, become more complex as a function of development. At the same time, they are not in constant flux. Rather, they tend to remain fairly stable in terms of the attachment relationship (secure or insecure) they reflect and are somewhat resistant to change (Bretherton & Munholland 1999).

Infants will respond to particular situations in particular ways, based on their assessment of environmental factors and their assessment and expectations regarding their caregivers' presence and availability. Mary Ainsworth (1967) describes how infants generally turn to an attachment figure as a "secure base from which to explore" (Ainsworth, Blehar, Waters, & Wall 1978, 265) the environment. If the infant perceives the environment to be frightening or threatening, however, exploratory behavior will decrease. Further, if the infant experiences the caregiver as unavailable or unresponsive, thus triggering the attachment behavioral system, exploratory behavior will decrease.

Bowlby appreciated Ainsworth's language of "secure base" and elaborated the sense in which he uses the term.

> This brings me to a central feature of my concept of parenting—the provision by both parents of a secure base from which a child or an adolescent can make sorties into the outside world and to which he can return knowing for sure that he will be welcomed when he gets there, nourished physically and emotionally, comforted if distressed, reassured if frightened. In essence this role is one of being available, ready to respond when called upon to encourage and perhaps assist, but to intervene actively only when clearly necessary. . . . In the case of children and adolescents we see them, as they get older, venturing steadily further from base and for increasing spans of time. The more confident they are that their base is secure and, moreover, ready if called upon to respond, the more they take it for granted. Yet should one or other parent become ill or die, the immense significance of the base to the emotional equilibrium of the child or adolescent or young adult is at once apparent. (1988, 11)

Attachment Theory and Corinne

After the death of his beloved wife, Joy, Christian writer and teacher C. S. Lewis wrote, "No one ever told me that grief felt so like fear" (1961, 1). From an attachment perspective, the linkage of grief and fear makes perfect sense. Separation from one's attachment figure can trigger great anxiety, and the permanent loss of this figure can shake one at the most basic level, leaving one feeling scared and adrift for a time. For someone with an insecure style of attachment, the loss may take an even greater toll, confirming one's expectations that life offers little safety and security. I believe this is an important part of Corinne's grief experience.

From Corinne's earliest days, her primary attachment figures were not consistently available to her. They were not a secure base for her and did not fulfill Bowlby's definition of caregiver responsiveness, which is the "willingness to act as comforter and protector" (1973, 201). Corinne's birth father largely disappeared from her life, becoming quite literally unavailable to her. Her mother, while more available, was inconsistent in her care for and responsiveness to Corinne. Theresa's decision to marry Walter and no longer live with Corinne was utterly devastating to Corinne. Walter, who might have functioned as a secure attachment figure for Corinne, instead rebuffed her efforts at closeness and ultimately rejected her. Corinne's aunt and uncle offered her some consistency of availability and care, but this, too, was compromised. Her aunt was passive and timid, sometimes leaving Corinne unsupported. Her uncle doted on Corinne but was sometimes harsh, and he died when Corinne was just fourteen.

Thus, in the midst of these painful and complicated relationships, Corinne had no opportunity to develop a sense of secure attachment to anyone and instead developed what appears to be an anxious style of attachment. She learned early on that the important people in her life were inconsistent, often unavailable, and sometimes utterly rejecting of her. She experienced abandonment and betrayal. She describes how terribly painful it was to take in the reality that "sometimes the people you should be able to trust the most are the ones who hurt you the most." These early attachment relationships continue to influence Corinne's adult life, most likely due to the tenacity of her internal working models.

Corinne has come to understand the world as unpredictable and scary, and she understands that many people—particularly men—are not to be trusted. Corinne frequently talks of her longing to be in a close relationship with a man, but she avoids dating. She is afraid of being misunderstood, hurt, or utterly rejected by the man to whom she would give her heart. Once, reflecting on aspects of her upbringing, Corinne said, "I realize I go through life in a terribly cautious way. I have as much fear of living as I have of dying."

The death of her mother has been Corinne's worst fear come true. The precious threads of connection to her mother have been snapped. In language analogous to that of the "secure base," Corinne says that, without her mother, she now has no safety net to catch her if she falls. Long after some aspects of her grief (e.g., intense sorrow and anger) have subsided, Corinne is left with a deep sense of disequilibrium. She feels scared and anxious in a way she does not fully understand, and she feels very alone.

Attachment to God

Theologian Gordon Kaufman has suggested that, in terms of characteristics commonly ascribed to God, God may function as an "absolutely adequate attachment-figure" (1981, 67). Phillip Bennett, a pastoral psychotherapist, has also pursued this theoretical linkage between attachment theory and relationship with God. He suggests the idea that when God functions as the ultimate secure base, people may better negotiate separation and loss.

> Without God as our secure base, our love of others easily becomes distorted by our fear of loss: we cling to others for fear of losing them (which may, in fact, drive them away, fulfilling our worst fear). Or we may try to avoid the pain of loss by avoiding intimacy altogether. . . . The secure base of God's love will not take away our losses but it can help us discover an abiding Presence that sustains us even in the midst of things that are passing away. In letting ourselves be loved by God, we form an attachment to the only One who cannot leave us. (1997, 31)

The application of attachment theory to people's relationship with God and the idea of God as the ultimate secure base are rich and exciting territories for study. Indeed, clinical psychologist and professor Kenneth Pargament suggests that attachment to God may represent an important and largely neglected "psycho-religious construct" for understanding people's relationship with God (personal communication, 1999). Professor and researcher Lee Kirkpatrick is at the very forefront of exploring the territory of attachment to God. Kirkpatrick (1999, 2005) suggests that attachment theory is an important (although not exhaustive or comprehensive) psychological framework for understanding religious experience because a personal relationship with God is at the core of monotheistic religions, especially Christianity. He maintains that believers of non-Christian traditions also often have personal relationships with their gods or other deities. He posits that, for many people, one's perceived relationship with God is at the core of one's religious beliefs, and this perceived relationship provides a form of love like that present in the infant-mother relationship.

Kirkpatrick considers various features of religion and religious behavior that may reflect a dynamic attachment process, such as images of God and the nature of religious love. I will here present one of his proposals, which draws on the work of attachment researcher Mary Ainsworth, mentioned above. Ainsworth (1985) denotes five criteria that distinguish attachment relationships from other relationships. The relationship between an infant and a caregiver constitutes an attachment if the infant (1) seeks proximity to the caregiver, (2) turns to the caregiver as a haven of safety at times of distress, (3) uses the caregiver as a secure base from which to explore the environment, (4) experiences anxiety when separation from the caregiver is threatened, and (5) experiences grief when the caregiver is lost. Kirkpatrick maintains that these same five criteria are satisfied when one considers religious beliefs and behaviors as part of the attachment behavioral system.

For example, Kirkpatrick proposes that many religious beliefs (e.g., the belief of many religions that God is always present and attentive) and religious behaviors (e.g., the uplifted arms, often part of Pentecostal worship services, that resemble infants waiting to be picked up by their mothers) reflect features of actual attachment processes that are intended to achieve proximity to God. Religious beliefs and behaviors intended to seek and maintain proximity to God may be considered part of the attachment behavioral system.

Also, Kirkpatrick considers ways in which religious beliefs and behaviors seem intended to seek God as a haven of safety in times of distress or crisis, Ainsworth's second criterion. This connection seems particularly strong in the case of prayer. For example, many researchers have noted that prayer and other religious behaviors tend to become more frequent after a significant death.[4] Kirkpatrick (1999) maintains that the attachment system may be activated by a significant death and thus generate certain attachment behaviors, including prayer. This is quite likely a part of what occurred in the United States following the terrorist attacks of September 11, 2001. Immediately after the horrifying events and terrible deaths, church attendance in this country went up, perhaps as people sought God as a haven of safety in their fear and distress. Interestingly, within two months rates of church attendance seemed to have returned to preattack levels (Goodstein 2001).

Further, Kirkpatrick considers ways in which religious beliefs portray God as the ultimate secure base, Ainsworth's third criterion for attachment relationships. For example, God is often portrayed or described as omnipresent and omniscient, qualities that would seem to offer ultimate security. While research has focused less on the function of religious beliefs in providing a secure base than on their function in providing a haven of safety in times of distress, one can look to many commonly ascribed attributes of God or other deities to discern the "secure base" feature. For example, the Hebrew and Christian Scriptures contain such descriptions. Kirkpatrick (2005) gives the example of the psalms, especially Psalm 23, where the description of God is analogous to that of the secure base. God is clearly a source of great security in these beautiful lines:

> Even though I walk through the darkest valley,
>   I fear no evil;
> for you are with me;
>   your rod and your staff—
>   they comfort me. (v. 4)

Having proposed ways in which many religious beliefs and behaviors seem to reflect the normative processes of the attachment behavioral system, Kirkpatrick (1992, 1999, 2005; Kirkpatrick & Shaver 1990) also considers individual differences in these processes, and he proposes two contrasting hypotheses in this regard. First, he proposes his "correspondence hypothesis" (2005, 102); in its basic form, this hypothesis posits that there is a fundamental correspondence or consistency between one's general style of attachment to human attachment figures and one's style of attachment to God. That is, one who is generally secure in attachment to others will feel security in attachment to God:

> Likewise, an "avoidant" orientation toward close relationships may be expected to manifest itself in the religious realm as agnosticism or atheism, or in a view of God as remote and inaccessible. Finally, an "ambivalent" orientation may find expression in a deeply emotional, all-consuming, and "clingy" relationship to God. (Kirkpatrick 1999, 809)

The proposed mechanism generating this correspondence across human and divine attachments is that of the internal working models of attachment that a person brings to any attachment relationship (Kirkpatrick 2005). Some studies support this correspondence hypothesis.[5] Some researchers have demonstrated a correspondence in children and adolescents between their attachment relationships and religious beliefs.[6] Other researchers have demonstrated this same correspondence, among both adults and children, in cross-cultural samples.[7]

In considering individual differences in the attachment processes that may be part of some religious beliefs and behaviors, Kirkpatrick offers a second hypothesis. He proposes that, in some cases, there will not exist a correspondence between one's human attachments and one's attachment to God, but God will function instead as a substitute attachment figure who compensates for one's human attachment figures (Kirkpatrick 1992, 1999, 2005; Kirkpatrick & Shaver 1990).[8] In developing this "compensation hypothesis" (Kirkpatrick 2005, 128), he suggests three sets of circumstances under which God may function in this way.

The first set of such circumstances involves situations of great stress or danger, when one's human attachment figures are not sufficiently present or powerful to protect one. One clear example of such situations is warfare; "only an all-powerful deity can offer a truly safe haven once the bullets start flying" (Kirkpatrick 1999, 812). Here is another powerful example. Recently, a survivor of the Rwandan genocide in 1994 shared in my grief and loss course how one group of Rwandan villagers gathered in their local church as they were being hunted by killers, some of whom were family and friends. They knew that they would not survive, but they wanted to be in God's house when they died. Interestingly, numerous researchers have concluded that "sudden religious conversions are most likely during times of severe emotional distress and crisis" (Kirkpatrick 1999, 812).[9]

A second set of circumstances under which one may turn to God as a substitute attachment figure is when one's primary attachment figure is "situationally unavailable" (Kirkpatrick 1999, 813). This link may be especially pronounced in situations in which the attachment figure is permanently separated or lost, such as through death. Thus, an adolescent whose parents have died or become completely unavailable in some other way may turn to God in an intense way to provide security and comfort no longer available from the parents.

A third set of circumstances is when one has a history of insecure attachments. Kirkpatrick and Shaver (1990) demonstrate that a history of insecure childhood attachments does correlate with the development of strong religiousness during adolescence or adulthood. They provide evidence that children who have insecure attachments to their parents may turn to God as a secure, substitute attachment figure who compensates for the lack of security in their parental attachments. Researcher Pehr Granqvist and Kirkpatrick (2004) have performed a meta-analysis of numerous studies that have considered the correlation between sudden religious conversions and the converts' history of parental attachments. Across these various studies, rates of conversion are significantly correlated with insecurity of either maternal or paternal attachment. One may also turn to God in this way in order to compensate for inadequate romantic relationships in adulthood (Kirkpatrick 1999).

Intriguingly, Kirkpatrick and others have provided empirical data that support both the correspondence and the compensation hypotheses with regard to God as an attachment figure, although statistically, correspondence appears to be the more common pattern (Kirkpatrick 2005). Further research is needed to tease out more fully the features of persons or circumstances that may lead toward either correspondence or compensation, as well as the possible endurance and effects of these patterns. Although certain critiques and challenges could be applied to Kirkpatrick's work,[10] his rich and innovative research makes abundantly clear that the concept of God as an attachment figure—either corresponding or compensatory—deserves ongoing and substantive consideration. We are only at the threshold of understanding the possible structures, features, and functions of this ultimate attachment relationship.

Attachment to God and Corinne

Consistent with Kirkpatrick's correspondence hypothesis, Corinne seems to have developed an anxious style of attachment to God. Most likely due to her internal working models of inconsistency in human relationships, Corinne experiences God as inconsistently accessible and responsive to her. Throughout her life, including after her mother's death, she has continued to pray to God nightly, and she describes feeling that she has some sort of connection with God that is important to her. At the same time, she describes not really knowing what sort of connection this is and to what sort of God she is praying. In Corinne's experience, God is male, and she was warned from her earliest years that most men are not to be trusted. Her uncle issued this warning about men, and he himself may have provided a model for God as angry, harsh, and guilt inducing. Also, as Corinne was growing up and faithfully saying her nightly prayers, God did not spare her from being utterly abandoned by her mother and utterly rejected by Walter. Even worse, God did not answer any of her prayers for her mother's healing. While Corinne wants to believe in a loving, faithful God, she now fears that God could actually be abandoning and even punishing. She talks of how very painful, overwhelming, and mysterious life can be at times and her confusion about the presence or absence of God in the midst of tragedy. Corinne has not internalized a sense of God in a way that brings her comfort or a sense of ultimate security in the midst of painful loss. God is not a secure base for her and does not tether her in the wake of her mother's death.

Ministerial Perspective

From a ministerial perspective, what sort of care and companioning might be most helpful to Corinne? I propose three ways in which a minister who considers Corinne's experience from an attachment perspective might be helpful to her. None of these are therapeutic stances or interventions. They are simply human, ministerial responses to the suffering of another.

First, a minister can offer understanding. Without an attachment perspective, we might be confused or baffled by some of Corinne's struggles and anxieties. She has been successful in her professional life and has many warm friendships. It has been two years since her mother died, and after all, loss is a part of life. Why, then, does she continue to carry such fear and existential anxiety? With an attachment perspective, we may understand why Corinne lives with chronic fear and anxiety and why her mother's death has left her feeling so ungrounded. We may also understand why her relationship with God does not help her to feel tethered in an ultimate sense.

Second, a minister can offer acceptance. We do not choose our styles of attachment; in a very real way, they choose us. An attachment perspective allows us to eschew any judgment we may feel when we hear of someone's persistent struggles and to offer instead a full and embracing acceptance. This may be especially important in the area of attachment to God. For example, ministers may sometimes experience discomfort when they hear someone describe their experience of God in ways that are unappealing or troubling. Some ministers may feel the impulse either to "defend" God in the face of such troubling descriptions or to "fix" the person's inadequate understanding of God. An attachment perspective helps us to see that we come by our style of attachment to God quite honestly, often based on our internal working models of human attachments. Our style of attachment to God is not something to be judged. It is something to be accepted. It is not a flaw or deficit in faith. It is a mark of our humanity.

At the same time, we would not want Corinne to believe she must always suffer such fear and anxiety. We would want her to hope that she will come to know the God of love, who has counted every hair on her head and cherishes her deeply. Therefore, the third thing a minister can offer Corinne is hope. Corinne is not fated always to suffer insecurity in attachment. Over time, the fear and anxiety with which she now lives may yield to a fundamental sense of safety and security. And both the minister and the faith community may be able to play an instrumental role in this development. Bowlby believes that a psychoanalyst can help a patient to move over time toward greater security in attachment by functioning as a secure base, "from which he [the patient] can explore the various unhappy and painful aspects of his life, past and present, many of which he finds it difficult or perhaps impossible to think about and reconsider without a trusted companion to provide support, encouragement, sympathy, and, on occasion, guidance" (1988, 138).

Ministers, too, may function as a secure base for their parishioners, not by offering psychotherapy but by offering *consistency of care and consistency of message*. Ministers have the great privilege of communicating God's abiding love and care for all God's people. They also model this in their interactions with others and encourage the faith community to do the same.

Members of the faith community—both individually and collectively—may also provide this consistency of care and consistency of message. For instance, a lay pastoral caregiving group in the parish could become a critical secure base for Corinne, offering both accessibility and responsiveness as she wrestles with her grief and her guilt.[11] Over time and through her experiences with her minister and with her faith community, Corinne may begin to internalize the reality that God is faithful in love, and this could utterly transform her life. In fact, over the course of my conversations with Corinne, during which I tried to model something of God's faithful care, she did indeed move toward greater security in attachment to God, even describing a vivid and deeply moving dream in which she clearly heard the words, "You are a child of God." While ministers and faith communities will never be perfect in these goals, they may still help people to feel something of the "perfect love [that] casts out fear" (1 John 4:18).

The Mosaic of Grief

An understanding of attachment theory, including attachment to God, can help a minister to appreciate the great intricacy of the mosaic of grief. From an attachment perspective, it is not overstatement to say that our responses to loss in adulthood may have their origins in our earliest moments of life. While one's mosaic of grief is fashioned by all aspects of one's life, one's style of attachment permeates the mosaic in an elemental way, like the finest particles comprising the mosaic materials themselves. One's style of attachment—to God and to others—may then shape or color other aspects of one's experience of grief. For instance, in the next chapter we will look at the critical area of meaning-making following loss. The meanings one derives from great loss may be a function—at least in part—of one's style of attachment. As Corinne seeks meaning in her mother's death, one troubling meaning with which she struggles is that her mother's untimely death may have been God's punishment for Corinne's selfishness. This meaning derives directly from her anxious attachment to God and colors her experience of grief. Only with an attachment perspective can we understand this vital dimension of her mosaic of grief.

All of our relationships may contribute to the mosaic of grief that takes shape after loss. Ministers and faith communities have the great opportunity to influence this shaping in ways that lead to healing and wholeness. With an attachment perspective, ministers may appreciate some of the finest nuances of one's grieving and may then offer understanding, acceptance, and hope.

And what sustains ministers in offering this understanding, acceptance, and hope? Ideally, perhaps, we are sustained by our own trust and hope that "we love because [God] first loved us" (1 John 4:19). Of course, trust and hope that God first loved us are harder to access and embrace if one's own experience of attachment to God has been marked by insecurity. As you have read and reflected on attachment theory in this chapter, perhaps you have wondered about your own style of attachment to others and to God. Perhaps various aspects of Corinne's experience and struggles have felt familiar, even if only vaguely so. Given how very critical our attachments are in the experience of grief, I invite you to spend some time with the reflection questions that follow. These questions invite you to reflect on your experience of important attachment relationships, both early in your life and now. The questions also invite you to consider how an understanding of attachment theory could inform your ministry to those who are grieving.

◆ ◆ ◆

Questions for Reflection

1. Think about your earliest attachment relationships, to your parents or to other primary caregivers. How would you describe these relationships in terms of the security and consistency they offered you? Think about your earliest sense of attachment to God. How would you describe your early relationship with God in terms of the security and consistency God seemed to offer you? Do you see any connections between your attachment relationships in early childhood and your attachment relationship with God?

2. At this point in your life, how would you describe your style of attachment to others? How would you describe your style of attachment to God? How might your style of attachment—to others and to God—influence your ways of ministering to others?

3. Think about your own experiences of loss and grief. How has your grief been shaped or affected by your attachments to others and your attachment to God? For example, have you felt securely "held" by others and/or by God in your grief? Have you, like Corinne, felt very alone and afraid in your grief? Have others or God functioned as a secure base for you when you have faced loss and grief? Has God been "an abiding Presence that sustains . . . even in the midst of things that are passing away" (Bennett 1997, 31)?

4. Think of grieving people to whom you have ministered or are ministering now. How might an attachment perspective shed light on some of their struggles? How might an attachment perspective shed light on your questions or struggles in ministering to them?

5. If Corinne sought your help and support, how might you respond to her, both initially and over time?

6. How might Corinne's faith community respond to her in ways that could lead to greater security of attachment?

7. What questions or ideas flowing from this chapter might you want to bring to your prayer or to conversations with trusted friends or colleagues?

4

Meaning-Making
after Loss

IF WE HAD to capture in one word what has become perhaps the essential feature of the contemporary grief field, I would choose the word _meaning_. Important contemporary grief theory describes the affirmation and/or reconstruction of meaning after loss as "the central process" in the experience of grief (Neimeyer 2001b, xii).[1] The realm of meaning has not always been central in grief theory and care. For instance, as we saw in chapter 2, Freud's (1957 [1917]) work on grief focuses primarily on the movement of psychic energy following loss: withdrawing it from the deceased person and investing it in new relationships. The various stage theories of grief have emphasized the seemingly instinctual and largely invariant sequence of responses to loss.

Significant contemporary work has moved away from traditional psychoanalytic and stage theories of grief and now asserts the centrality of meaning-making in grief. New psychoanalytic theory also emphasizes this feature, understanding mourning as "a crisis of meaning" (Hagman 2001, 22). At the very forefront of this contemporary perspective is Robert Neimeyer, a constructivist psychologist. This chapter presents the work of Neimeyer and other grief theorists who are doing important work on meaning and grief. A case vignette invites us into the territory of meaning.

Case Vignette

David is a sixty-year-old retired businessman. He and his sister grew up in a stable and loving home in the Midwest, and their parents were happily married for sixty-two years until their father died two years ago at ninety-one. David's mother is a healthy ninety-year-old, still living in the home in which she raised her children. David's parents grew up during the Great Depression, and they witnessed the sheer grit and hard work that survival required. As a child, David frequently heard about the importance of working hard, being self-sufficient, and taking care of one's family. David's father served in World War II and sustained a serious leg injury. Despite the persistent effects of this injury, he spent the rest of his working life as an appliance repairman and was utterly devoted to his family. David's mother felt that her most important purpose in life was to care for her husband and her children. David's parents were faithful members of their church, and they raised their children to believe in a powerful but distant God who rewards those who do His will. David grew up hearing, "God helps those who help themselves," and he watched his parents live out their part of that equation. He also frequently heard, "Ask and it shall be given to you," and his family prayed regularly both at church and at home for health and happiness. David's father retired at sixty-five, and he and David's mother then enjoyed close to twenty-five wonderful years of retirement, until David's father's illness and death.

From a young age, David felt that his most important life goal was to create and be devoted to a loving family, and he planned accordingly. Wanting to be self-sufficient in supporting a family, he was a business major in college with a goal of owning his own business by the time he was thirty. Through tenacity and lots of hard work, David met this goal. David and Janet had been high school sweethearts who shared a vision of family life, and they married when they were twenty-five. Within five years, they had three beautiful children.

The next twenty years seemed to fly by for David. He worked hard in his business and experienced inevitable stress as the economy rose and fell. For the most part, though, his hard work paid off. He and Janet were able to buy a lovely house in a town with good schools. Their children were happy and involved in numerous activities. As the children grew, David and Janet got busier and busier, volunteering in sports programs and school activities. They were active in their church community, and they also sought ways to help others. Janet organized the food distribution program in their church, and they made sizable donations to charity. Janet and David felt very blessed, and they thanked God every week at church for all they enjoyed.

Before they knew it, their children were off to college. As they saw the empty nest fast approaching, David and Janet began to talk about the next phase of their lives. Like his father, David planned to retire at sixty-five. He would sell his business, and then he and Janet would begin a long and wonderful retirement. For many years, they had spent summer vacations in the mountains with their children, and they dreamed of building a special retirement home there where their children and grandchildren would gather for every holiday. They met with a financial planner and began saving for this dream.

When Janet was fifty, she felt tired and lethargic and began losing weight. When these symptoms did not abate, she saw her doctor, who ordered some medical tests. When the results came back, David and Janet felt the bottom drop out of their world. Janet had cancer. They immediately saw specialists, who were quite hopeful. This was treatable, although it would take a lot out of Janet. The next few months did indeed take their toll on Janet as she underwent both radiation and chemotherapy. They prayed every day that God would heal Janet, and their church community also prayed weekly for her healing. Throughout the ordeal, David and Janet clung together, and they comforted each other with talk of their retirement dreams. After several months of treatment, the cancer went into remission, and Janet was given a hopeful prognosis. Janet, David, and the children celebrated her recovery. They toasted life, and they thanked God for healing Janet.

Life soon resumed its busy pace. All three of their children graduated from college and began careers. Two of their children got married, and within a few years the first grandchildren appeared on the scene. David and Janet were ecstatic and thanked God for all their blessings. They purchased the land on which they planned to build their retirement home, and they spent many wonderful evenings imagining the layout of the home. At fifty-eight, Janet began to feel ill again. With terror in their hearts, they returned to the hospital for tests. The cancer was back, and it had spread. Less hopeful this time, the specialists suggested more aggressive treatments, which Janet and David quickly embraced. Their family and church community resumed prayers for Janet's healing. David began to talk about retiring soon, and Janet agreed. Within a few months, David had found a buyer for his business. He also hired builders to begin construction of their retirement home. Through the months of treatment, David distracted Janet with construction stories and design ideas. They planned their home down to the smallest detail, and Janet told the children that Christmas would be celebrated in the new house. Around Thanksgiving, though, Janet took a turn for the worse. The specialists said there was no more they could do. Janet was dying. David and the children spent every possible minute with Janet, and they were with her when she died in mid-December.

At first David got through his days by keeping very busy. He established a memorial fund in Janet's name, with the proceeds going to cancer research. He spoke daily with the builders of their retirement home, tracking every detail and making sure it was exactly as Janet and he had wanted. He spent time with his children and grandchildren. But now, the busyness has stopped. His business is sold. The retirement home is finished. And the children are busy with work and family obligations. For the first time in his life, David feels utterly lost. He does not know what his life is about anymore. His lifelong goal of being a successful businessman and raising a family is done. His dreams of retirement make no sense without Janet. The future he imagined is dashed, with nothing to take its place. He is struggling to figure out what his purpose in life now is. David is also struggling to figure out where God has been in the midst of all that has happened. David grew up hearing, "God helps those who help themselves," and he took this to heart. No one has worked harder than he has, and yet he feels God did not do His part to save Janet. He also believed in the promise, "Ask and it shall be given to you," and he does not understand why the countless prayers for Janet's healing did not work. David is not sure where God was in this terrible time. None of it makes any sense, and David is wondering how to go on with the rest of his life.

The Meaning of *Meaning*

As David struggles to make sense of what has happened, to figure out what his purpose in life now is, and to understand where God has been in all of this, we could say that he is experiencing a crisis of meaning. But what does that mean? What is the meaning of *meaning*? *Meaning* is a common word; we hear it all the time. For instance, many people talk about wanting to do something *meaningful* with their lives, and this is sometimes the basis for the career or vocational choices people make or volunteer work in which they engage. We hold on to treasured items because they *mean* something to us. For some people, the search for a *meaningful* relationship is an important quest. And many parents name the raising of children as the greatest source of *meaning* in their lives.

Despite such common uses, the meaning of *meaning* is often vague or fuzzy. Authors define it in a variety of ways, and sometimes not at all. Given the centrality of *meaning* in the contemporary grief field, it is essential that we bring some clarity to this concept. We can begin with a cartoon from *The New Yorker* (Jan. 19, 2004, 60) in which a well-dressed, middle-aged woman is shopping in a fancy boutique and asks the saleswoman, "What would you suggest to fill the dark, empty spaces in my soul?" We could say that this woman is searching for meaning. All of us at one time or another must confront the dark, empty, frightening, or mysterious spaces in our own lives and in the world. We must ask the largest, most difficult questions of life, such as "Who am I?" "Why was I born?" "What is the purpose or goal of my life?" "Why does the world work the way it does?" "Why is there so much suffering?" "Is there a God?" "What if there is no God?" David is struggling with some of these painful questions.

The answers we shape to these questions and others like them are expressions of meaning. From the German root *meinen*, which is "to think," meaning is the deep sense we make of things, the way we understand the world, how we articulate the overarching purpose or goal of our lives, the significance we seek in living, the core values by which we order our lives. Meaning also includes theological dimensions such as how we understand God's activity in the world, God's feelings about and responses to us, and God's role in suffering.

Meaning, including theological meaning, helps to create order, sense, and purpose out of experiences and events that could otherwise seem random, nonsensical, disordered, or chaotic. Perhaps in large part for this reason, humans seem driven to seek meaning. Psychiatrist and concentration camp survivor Viktor Frankl describes the search for meaning as the primary motivation of humanity; when this drive is thwarted, one faces an "existential vacuum" (1984 [1959], 111) and sees life as without meaning and purpose. Today, Robert Neimeyer describes humans as "inveterate meaning makers" (1999, 67). In our search for meaning, we are influenced by many sources. Culture plays an enormous role in shaping meaning.[2] For instance, one's culture often dictates what is most valued in life, such as communal relationships or material success. Meaning may also be shaped by families, communities, educational systems, social structures, and religions. Given this variety of sources, each person finds and fashions meaning in ways particular to him or her. *no single meaning!*

Stories and Meaning

There are various roads to understanding and articulating meaning in our lives, but an essential one is narrative or story. Human life is fundamentally grounded in stories.[3] Although cognitive and developmental psychologists continue to debate whether storytelling is an innate or learned skill, we do know that from the age of three or so, children in most cultures can shape rudimentary stories themselves (Polkinghorne 1988). This skill gets more complex as a function of age and development. We frequently communicate by way of stories, and over time we come to understand ourselves, others, and the world largely through stories. And it seems that it has always been so. Early humans drew pictures on cave walls to tell stories. Ancient Egyptian burial crypts are covered with storytelling symbols. What we know of Socrates is due largely to the storytelling of his pupil Plato. What we know of the historical Jesus of Nazareth is largely drawn from the storytelling of the New Testament writers. "The narratives of the world are without number. . . . [T]he narrative is present at all times, in all places, in all societies; the history of narrative begins with the history of mankind; there does not exist, and never has existed, a people without narratives" (Barthes 1966, cited in Polkinghorne 1988, 14).

Stories or narratives come in many forms, such as "personal and social histories, myths, fairy tales, novels, and the everyday stories we use to explain our own and others' actions" (Polkinghorne 1988, 1). So extensive are the many varieties of stories in our lives that we may not be consciously aware of their presence much of the time. But let's imagine a possible day in one's life and notice the presence of stories. On a Monday morning, Sandra goes to work. She listens to some news stories on the radio during her commute. At the watercooler, colleagues ask her about her weekend, and she tells them a story or two. She then listens to their stories of weekend adventures or misadventures. At a team meeting later that morning, the manager tells the story of the company's history, its recent struggles, and its plans to reinvent itself to become more competitive. At lunch, Sandra meets her friend Barbara, and they catch up on recent events in their lives. At dinner that night, Sandra, her husband, Bill, and their children each share some stories from their day. As she puts her young children to bed, Sandra reads them their favorite story. She and Bill then watch a television drama. Later, before falling asleep, Sandra reads the next chapter of a terrific science-fiction novel. Sandra's day was filled with stories, her own and those of others.

We are people of stories. And this pertains to our faith lives as well. Scripture begins with a creation story. From there unfold the stories of kings, prophets, tribes, wars, brave women, suffering, victories. The Christian faith draws on these stories while centering on the compelling story of the life, ministry, death, and resurrection of Jesus Christ, and the ongoing presence of Christ in our midst through his Spirit. This is the narrative that Christians have been telling and retelling for thousands of years. When we gather with our faith communities, we are hearing and telling the story again. In religious education, we are making sure that all of us know and understand the story. This Christian commitment to story is reflected in the lyrics of two wonderful hymns. The first is the old-time favorite:

> I love to tell the story, 'twill be my theme in glory,
> To tell the old, old story of Jesus and His love.
> (A. K. Hankey, "I Love to Tell the Story," 1866)

The second hymn, a more recent one, goes like this:

> We come to share our story.
> We come to break the bread.
> We come to know our rising from the dead.
> (D. Haas, "Song of the Body of Christ," 1989)

What is the connection between stories and meaning? First, let's recall how we defined meaning above. Meaning is the deep sense we make of things, the way we understand the world, how we articulate the overarching purpose or goal of our lives, the significance we seek in living, the core values by which we order our lives.]Meaning also includes theological dimensions, such as how we understand God's activity in the world, God's feelings about and responses to us, and God's role in suffering. Meaning, including theological meaning, helps to create order, sense, and purpose out of what could otherwise seem random, nonsensical, disordered, or chaotic. A primary way that we learn and communicate meaning is through stories (Mishler 1986; Polkinghorne 1988). Stories create meaning and reflect meaning. Familial, cultural, and theological meaning is often embedded in stories. For example, family stories may teach the value of hard work or of placing family relationships above all. Stories from various cultures may inculcate the importance of self-sufficiency or of honoring the elderly. Faith stories may emphasize Jesus' love for little children or the need to repent of sin. From all of the stories we hear, we begin to learn what is of value and how to make sense of life. These stories become important sources of meaning in our lives.

The Common Elements of Stories

We communicate by means other than stories. For instance, if someone asks us for our phone number or e-mail address, we may simply share information, without a story. We might engage in a classroom or family discussion without embarking on a story. So what is a story, exactly, and what distinguishes it from other types of communication? Stories are comprised of some common elements.[4]

- ◆ *Plot.* Stories have plots. The plot of a story is what happens; it is the arranging and unfolding of events or moments from beginning to end.
- ◆ *Theme.* Stories are about something. If someone asks me what a story is about and I distill it down to a word or two, such as "honor" or "family secrets," I am giving the theme. The theme is the heart of a story. A story may have more than one theme.
- ◆ *Characters.* Stories often have a main character, the protagonist, and other characters who assume various roles. Some stories have an antagonist who makes life difficult for the protagonist in some way.

- *Time and Timing.* Stories unfold in time. In most stories, there is a clear beginning ("Once upon a time . . .") and a clear ending ("And they all lived happily ever after. The end."). In between the beginning and the ending, things happen with a certain timing. One moment or detail or event is connected to the next, and that one to the next, and so on in a temporal sequence that provides a sense of order to the story's events.

- *Continuity.* As a story unfolds, it builds on itself, and there is continuity. For instance, if characters are introduced in chapter 1, they do not need to be reintroduced in chapters 2 and 3. If something has happened in the first chapter, this detail is carried forth and developed in subsequent chapters. The development of characters or unfolding of plot is continuous; past, present, and future are connected.

- *Sense/Coherence.* An essential dimension of stories is their sense or coherence. Usually, the plot unfolds in a way that makes logical sense. The details cohere or hang together well. The loose ends get tied up neatly and sensibly by the end. Even if we don't like a particular story, it may still make sense to us.

In any story, all of these elements work together to create the overall effect. If there is a problem with any of these elements, the "spell" of the story may be broken, and we can be left dissatisfied. For example, if an important character is introduced in one chapter and then never heard from again, we might be confused and frustrated. If a movie ends abruptly without tying together all the loose ends, we might be annoyed and wish we could get our money back. Perhaps our greatest discomfort is when stories just do not make any sense. In my first semester of college, I took a course in modern drama. I hated it. I had decided to become an English major because I enjoyed stories: of people's lives, of history, of the world. Up until that time, the stories I knew unfolded in ways I could follow, ways that made sense, even if they were surprising or unexpected. The plays we studied in the course were the antithesis of these things. The works of Samuel Beckett, Eugene Ionesco, and others did not seem to capture life as I knew it or could imagine it at all. I did not know how to relate to the characters or their stories. The culmination of my frustration came when we read Beckett's *Waiting for Godot*. I struggled with the nonsensical plot and bizarre characters. In one especially painful stretch of the play, the character Lucky (who is decidedly unlucky in the play) recites several pages of disjointed, unrelated words, including some made-up words. I didn't get it. I wanted to dump the play and the course. Interestingly, the professor gave us a choice of final assignment: we could write a paper on some aspect of modern drama, or we could memorize and recite to the class two pages of the gibberish from *Waiting for Godot*. In retrospect, I'm sure he gave us the choice as a joke, assuming that no one would choose to spend time memorizing gibberish. He didn't know how desperate I had become. Not knowing what I could write for a course that had utterly stymied me, I lunged for the alternate assignment like a struggling swimmer grasping for a lifeline. I was the only one who made this choice. I spent several days memorizing the string of nonsense words. It was incredibly difficult. I had to connect them in my mind either phonetically or by making up some sort of bizarre associations between them. In the final class, as I got ready for my recitation, I noticed the professor did not have his copy of the play opened, and I asked him, "Aren't you going to read along to make sure I get it right?" He said something to the effect of "It doesn't matter. The words don't make sense anyway."

As I reflect on this incident after many years, two insights emerge. First, I can now appreciate that the modern drama I studied did indeed "make sense." The writers were trying to communicate what they experienced as the absurdity or futility of life, where time means nothing and there is no point to anything. They portrayed this futility and meaninglessness through stories that made little sense. The logic or sense of what they were communicating was conveyed precisely through the non-sense of the stories themselves. Second, this incident made clear how critical *sense* often is. I could not tolerate stories that, at least on the surface, lacked all sense.

Our Stories and Loss

Stories are not just something we read or watch on television. Nor are they only what we learn from our families, cultures, and faith communities. Each of us also creates our own life stories. When we reflect on our lives, we often do so in the form of stories. We take the events of our lives and arrange them in particular ways, creating a plotline. We feature certain people as major or minor characters. Our stories often have themes. We order and shape the elements of our stories so that there is continuity, coherence, and sense to them. Our stories express the meaning of our lives. They reflect how we understand the sense, purpose, and significance of our lives. They communicate what we value, what our priorities in life are, and what we believe. Importantly, they express how we understand ourselves. Our stories often incorporate and reflect the meaning we have learned from other sources (family, culture, faith), although we may not always be aware of this. Not only do our stories reflect meaning we have learned, but they may also create new meaning. The way we arrange and interpret the elements of our lives may yield new and surprising meaning. Thus, our meaning system—both the meaning we learn and the meaning we create—is embedded in and expressed through our stories.

But what happens to our life story and our meaning system when we experience a significant loss? Loss can disrupt some or all of the elements of our story, thereby threatening our meaning system, including our sense of self (Neimeyer 1999, 2001a). For example, one may have imagined one's life to include a long marriage, children, and grandchildren; this anticipated plot can be ruined by the unanticipated loss of a divorce. The death of a child can devastate the timing of one's story; children are not supposed to die before their parents. When a certain loss occurs, one's life theme may no longer make sense. For example, the theme of "job success at all costs" may become senseless when one is disabled and no longer able to work. With disruption to the story comes the possibility of shaken meaning. How does one make sense of the loss when it does not fit one's story? How does one make sense of one's story now that the loss has occurred? This struggle for sense is reflected in common responses to loss, such as, "I don't know how to make sense of this," or "This just doesn't make any sense."

David's Story

From a young age, David fashioned a clear and consistent life story by which he has lived. Janet's death at a young age was never part of his story, and this event has profoundly threatened both his story and his meaning system. Let's consider the elements of David's story that have been disrupted by the death of Janet.

David and Janet carefully planned the *plot* of their lives, and it did not include Janet's untimely death; rather, they planned for a long and fulfilling retirement, as David's parents enjoyed. David's story never allowed for the disappearance of Janet, perhaps the most central *character* of his life. The primary *theme* by which David has shaped his life is that of "work hard and family first." At sixty, he finds himself with no work and with older children with lives of their own. He does not have a theme for the rest of his life. Janet's death has also ruptured the *timing* of David's story. She was not supposed to die young. With his parents as his model, David assumed they would live into their nineties, and that perhaps Janet would outlive him. Her death has shattered the *continuity* of his story. His imagined future was completely structured around their shared life. Now he does not know how to think about or move into the future; his future feels utterly disconnected from his past and present. Finally, David is struggling to make *sense* of Janet's death. His father's death at ninety-one, although sad, made sense to David; his father lived to a ripe old age and fulfilled his life's ambitions. And after all, no one lives forever. Janet's death, in contrast, makes no sense. It does not fit with his understanding of how the world is supposed to work and how his life is supposed to go. Janet's death has also disrupted theological dimensions of David's life story. David has lived by the theological theme of "God helps those who help themselves." He feels he has done his part, and he does not know where God was in Janet's suffering and why God did not spare Janet's life. It isn't fair. He has also relied on the theme of "Ask and it shall be granted to you," and yet all of the prayers for Janet's healing did not succeed. With Janet's death, David's story has imploded, and he is left, in essence, in narrative freefall. With the loss of his story, David's meaning system has been profoundly shaken.

Meaning-Making after Loss

David's painful situation is far from unusual. For all of us, loss can be an unwelcome intruder in our life narrative, potentially challenging, disrupting, and even decimating our overarching life story, our meaning system, and our very sense of self. Some contemporary grief theorists, including Robert Neimeyer, assert that challenges to one's meaning system go right to the heart of the grief experience; "grieving individuals can be viewed as struggling to affirm or reconstruct a personal world of meaning that has been challenged by loss" (Neimeyer, Prigerson, & Davies 2002, 239). According to this perspective, the central process of grieving is integrating the loss into one's story and sorting out what it all means. Let us look more closely at this process.

Everyone has a particular story, and everyone has a particular meaning system that is embedded in and expressed through this story. In some cases, one's story and meaning system can absorb a loss without being completely disrupted. In such a case, one eventually affirms one's meaning system, and grieving, while perhaps still very painful, ultimately involves the return to "something already established" (Attig 2001, 34). For example, when my grandmother died at 104, I was able to integrate this loss into my overarching life story quite readily. There was nothing shocking, untimely, or senseless about her death at such an advanced age, and my ways of understanding life and death were not threatened. Although I felt some sadness that my earthly relationship with her was over, her death in fact affirmed my meaning system, which includes the understanding that human beings should not live forever and the joy in knowing a loved one who has lived a long and faithful life has gone to God.

Clearly, such affirmation of meaning does not always occur after loss. In some circumstances, such as with David in our case vignette, one's story and one's meaning system may be disrupted or even destroyed by the loss, and grieving therefore requires the reconstruction of meaning. Neimeyer describes this process in narrative terms; in essence, one must consider one's story and perhaps revise and even rewrite parts of it so that it may once again provide sense, coherence, and continuity. "Like a novel that loses a central character in the middle chapters, the life story disrupted by loss must be reorganized, rewritten, to find a new strand of continuity that bridges the past with the future in an intelligible fashion" (Neimeyer 2001d, 263). This is the task that awaits David. The future he imagined with Janet by his side has disappeared, and he faces the need to make "attempts at reconstructing a life worth living" (Neimeyer & Keesee 1998, 237).

Meanings can and do change; for example, probably none of us think about life and loss in exactly the same ways now as we did when we were fifteen. But how does the reconstruction of meaning after loss happen, exactly? Let me offer three responses to this question. First, *the reconstruction of meaning after loss may occur by having more plot for one's narrative.* Some people suffer from shrunken or frozen narratives, particularly after loss. For instance, in Charles Dickens's classic *Great Expectations*, the elderly Miss Havisham lived a shrunken, frozen story. She was jilted on her wedding day and never recovered from this trauma. For the rest of her life, she remained in her deteriorating wedding dress as her wedding cake rotted in the corner. Her life narrative virtually froze at the moment of her great disappointment. All of us may suffer from shrunken or frozen stories after loss; the loss may foreclose our future story as we have imagined it, leaving us, in essence, outside of a story. This is what has happened to David in our vignette. To break the hold of a frozen story, one may need more plot for one's narrative. New plot material may stir and shift things, much as the flow of a warm-water current can melt surface ice. New plot material allows for an expanded—and expansive—story, with new possibilities for oneself and one's future. And with these new possibilities come potential new meanings. A critical role of therapists and other caring support people—including ministers—is sometimes to offer more plot for another's narrative.

Second, *the reconstruction of meaning after loss may occur through bringing new or altered interpretations to the loss event.* We know that any event or experience may be interpreted in a variety of ways. For example, think of the perennial question, "Is the glass half full or half empty?" The same glass may be interpreted in at least two ways, and each interpretation suggests a different meaning (e.g., whether one's situation is good or not so good). Let's consider this ancient Chinese short story:

> Once upon a time there was a Chinese farmer whose horse ran away, and all the neighbors came around to commiserate that evening. "So sorry to hear your horse has run away. This is most unfortunate." The farmer said, "Maybe." The next day the horse came back bringing seven wild horses with it, and everybody came back in the evening and said, "Oh, isn't that lucky. What a great turn of events. You now have

eight horses!" And the farmer said, "Maybe." The next day his son tried to break one of these horses and ride it, but he was thrown and broke his leg, and they all said, "Oh dear, that's too bad," and he said, "Maybe." The following day the conscription officers came around to conscript people into the army and they rejected his son because he had a broken leg. Again all the people came around and said, "Isn't that great!" And he said, "Maybe." (Watts 2006, 146)

Is the farmer lucky or unlucky? It depends on one's interpretation of events. According to a well-known expression, "We do not see things as they are. We see them as we are."[5] We tend to interpret events and experiences out of our own self-understanding, which is reflected in our narrative. When any aspects of our self-understanding shift, new interpretations may emerge. And new interpretations make possible new meanings.

Third, *the process of meaning reconstruction after loss cannot be separated from one's social and interpersonal world*; it contains an inherently relational dimension. For example, meanings are often co-constructed in relationship with others, as we tell and retell our stories (Neimeyer 2001a). The process of meaning-making "transcends us as individuals as we communicate our personal thoughts and experiences to others, and as we, in turn, participate as hearers and viewers of their expressions" (Polkinghorne 1988, 15–16).

The process of meaning reconstruction after loss may be both painful and painstaking. At the same time, it may be an opportunity for some to deconstruct or jettison a destructive life story in favor of a freer and more life-giving narrative. Narrative therapy has helped us to understand that parts of our life stories are handed to us by others, sometimes with deleterious results.[6] Many people believe rigid, oppressive, and destructive stories about themselves because of what they have been told. For example, a mother who struggles with shame in her own life may project this struggle onto her child through shaming words and behaviors; over time, the child becomes convinced that he is bad in some fundamental way, and this theme becomes the bedrock of both his story and his meaning system. By challenging our narratives and the meanings embedded therein, loss may create opportunities for new, fuller, and more satisfying stories and meanings.

Meaninglessness

Sadly, some people are unable either to affirm or to reconstruct meaning after loss, and they may find themselves in the most painful state of meaninglessness. Meaninglessness means the absence of all those things we have identified with meaning. It means "a pervasive sense of the absence of significance, direction, or purpose in one's life, life in general, or the entire world" (VandenBos 2007, 561). When one struggles with meaninglessness, there is no deep sense to the world or to one's life. One experiences life as random and disconnected rather than coherent. One feels a lack of purpose and direction in life. The writer of Ecclesiastes captures the lack of purpose and sense of futility that are part of meaninglessness:

> Vanity of vanities, says the Teacher, vanity of vanities! All is vanity. What do people gain from all the toil at which they toil under the sun? A generation goes, and a generation comes, but the earth remains forever. The sun rises and the sun goes down, and hurries to the place where it rises. The wind blows to the south, and goes around to the north; round and round goes the wind, and on its circuits the wind returns. All streams run to the sea, but the sea is not full; to the place where the streams flow, there they continue to flow. All things are wearisome; more than one can express; the eye is not satisfied with seeing, or the ear filled with hearing. What has been is what will be, and what has been done is what will be done; there is nothing new under the sun. (Eccl. 1:2-9)

Meaninglessness is a terrible thing. It may even be a death sentence. I recently spoke with a woman who did international crisis work following a devastating natural disaster in another country. Many parents lost their children in the disaster. Some of them then found life completely meaningless and committed suicide. Without a future story and without meaning, they did not know how to live. As award-winning author Barry Lopez has written, "Sometimes a person needs a story more than food to stay alive" (Lopez & Pohrt 1990, 48). *It's not by food or water... but by every word that comes from the father*

Meaning-Making in Theological Perspective

Why do some people experience profound "narrative disruptions" (Neimeyer 2000, 207) and threatened meaning after loss while others enjoy some essential continuity in both story and meaning system? Why do some people suffer frozen or shrunken stories after loss while others experience more narrative stability and flexibility? Why do some people affirm or reconstruct meaning after loss while others find themselves suffering meaninglessness? I propose that these questions—and the answers we fashion to them—are ultimately theological because they bring us eventually to our concepts of God. While meaning-making after loss is central to the contemporary secular grief field, I believe it is, in the end, a theological enterprise. How is this so?

 First, *everyone has a story, and concepts of God may shape each person's story in profound ways.* This is true also for atheists; their stories may be shaped by the lack of a concept of God or gods. We may not always be conscious of the God concepts—or lack thereof—that have shaped our stories. At times of crisis and loss, however, these concepts may emerge in high relief. William Willimon, an author and professor of Christian ministry, has written, "A great trauma makes theologians of us all" (2002, 104). That is, the experience of trauma may be so painful or jarring that it forces us to grapple with our deepest understandings of the world in order to make sense of it. These deepest understandings are ultimately theological. How we make ultimate sense of trauma—and I propose how we make ultimate sense of all loss—flows from and depends on how we conceive of God, God's activity in the world, and ourselves before God. Is there a God? What if there is no God? Is God to blame for one's loss and suffering? Does God cause or allow suffering to punish or teach lessons? Does God prevent suffering if one only prays hard enough? Is God powerless in the face of suffering? Is God moved deeply by suffering? Does God suffer with those who suffer? Does God care faithfully throughout one's suffering? These questions suggest very different concepts of God, and these different concepts will likely shape very different stories and meaning systems.

This leads to the second aspect of meaning-making as a theological enterprise: *different God concepts lead to different meanings, and theologically speaking, all meanings are* not *created equal.* To put it baldly, our concept of God may largely shape whether we dwell in hopeful meaning or desperate meaninglessness after loss. As we discussed above, parts of our life stories and meaning systems are handed to us from our families, cultures, and faith groups, sometimes with deleterious results. Some people are handed terrible stories and ideas about God. For instance, some women have been encouraged by their families, friends, and religious leaders to stay in abusive marriages because God forbids divorce (cf. Matt. 5:32; 19:9; Mark 10:11-12; Luke 16:18). Such counsel invites these women, their children, and their abusers to think of God as preferring violence, innocent suffering, trauma, and sometimes death over the dissolution of a marriage. Clearly, this counsel might be interpreted to suggest a concept of God as rigid, punishing, terrifying, and even sadistic. What sorts of meanings might this God concept yield? How will abused women and children understand their worth and dignity? How will they imagine their futures? What will they believe about their value in God's eyes? What will they pass on to their children and grandchildren about life, about marriage, about religion, and about God? Will they ultimately live in hopeful meaning or desperate meaninglessness? [7]

Different God concepts lead to different meanings, including the meaning we make of mystery. This is the third aspect of meaning-making as a theological enterprise. *Mystery is a constant character in the drama of grief and loss.*[8] For example, we are wrestling with mystery when we ponder why children develop terminal illnesses or why some people suffer so much. None of us can answer these questions fully. There is so much we cannot understand, and we are left with the mystery of it all. Even our faith falls short of wresting complete sense out of mystery, as the poet Lord Byron expressed in the following lines:

> I gazed (as oft I have gazed the same)
> To try if I could wrench aught out of death
> Which should confirm or shake or make a faith;
> But it was all a mystery.
> (*Don Juan* canto V, 1973, 228)

Sometimes in the face of mystery, people experience meaninglessness. Their meaning system, including their God concept, does not help them to embrace or accept the mystery of life, and the mystery of it all makes their suffering worse. David is struggling in this way. His concept of God does not help him to understand and accept Janet's illness and death; rather, his concept of God is fueling his struggle with meaninglessness.

In contrast, the Christian faith suggests that life, while full of mystery, is never meaningless. There is meaning in mystery. The Christian story is steeped in the Paschal mystery of Christ's suffering, death, and resurrection. And the heart of this mystery is love: God's fierce and faithful love for each person, manifest for all time in the life, death, and resurrection of Jesus Christ. "For God so loved the world that he gave his only Son, so that everyone who believes in him may not perish but may have eternal life" (John 3:16). While life can seem scary and senseless in times of loss, its deepest meaning issues from a faithful God whose ways we can't fully know but who is love. We cannot make human sense of every loss, but God is love (1 John 4:8, 16). This love provides ultimate sense and ultimate meaning in the face of mystery. With this understanding, we may be freed from the need to seek meaning in human terms and instead surrender to what is perhaps the greatest paradox of the Christian life: there is suffering, *and* God is love; there is pain, *and* God is love; there is loss, *and* God is love; there is mystery, *and* God is love. We have never been promised that we will not suffer, but we have been assured that nothing will ever "separate us from the love of God in Christ Jesus our Lord" (Rom. 8:39). I once heard the acceptance of this paradox expressed by a young man whose father had recently died. This man was struggling to understand the meaning of his father's death but felt God deeply and lovingly present to him in his struggle. He said, "I think the meaning of my father's death is that perhaps I don't need to find meaning in it. I can just let it be."

Meaning and Attachment to God

In the last chapter, we explored at length the area of attachment to God and the possible effects of one's attachment to God on one's grief experience. How might meaning-making after loss be connected to one's style of attachment to God? I suggest that our story and our meaning system—including our God concept and our understanding of ultimate meaning—are deeply connected to our attachment to God. With a secure attachment to God, we may have a fundamental sense of trust, security, and safety. When the winds of loss howl around us, our story and our meaning system may fundamentally hold. With God as a secure base, we may better tolerate the unfairness, randomness, and mystery of life. There is meaning in mystery, and the ultimate meaning is love. While we grieve deeply for those we have loved and lost, we are not plunged into despair. We are tethered in an ultimate sense to a loving, cherishing God who holds us and protects us from the threat of meaninglessness. Without such security in attachment to God, our story may be fundamentally rocked by loss, leaving us in narrative freefall. We may search and struggle for new meaning that we may or may not find. We may experience God as inconsistent, unavailable, or unresponsive, even in our great need. We may not feel held by love, and we may struggle to figure out God's role in our suffering and loss. The mystery of life may be profoundly disturbing to us, and we may be at particular risk for meaninglessness after loss.

Ministerial Perspective

From a ministerial perspective, what sort of care and companioning might be most helpful to David? First, a minister can care for David's story. Everyone has a story, and our stories express what we believe about ourselves, about life, and about God. Therefore, people's stories—like their very selves—deserve care. Mary Pellauer, in *God's Fierce Whimsy*, says, "I have a very deep sense that there is nothing more beautiful than listening to people tell their stories about faith and God. They express, as nothing else can, who we really are, and what we really believe in, and the meaning in our lives. . . . If there's anything worth calling theology, it is listening to people's stories—listening to them and honoring and cherishing them" (Cannon et al. 1985, 133). The need to care for stories is particularly great after loss; people are often most vulnerable when they are struggling with disrupted narratives and threatened meaning. This is the case with David. He lived a clear and coherent story until Janet's illness and death; he is now suffering from terrible narrative disruption and the threat of meaninglessness. He is confused about God. He feels that God did not respond to him in the ways he had always expected. He does not feel God's love in the midst of his suffering. David needs to tell and perhaps retell his story, and he needs compassionate understanding of the painful narrative struggle he is enduring.

Second, a minister can help David to expand his narrative and to shape new meaning in order to live with hope into his future. We might help David to expand his story by offering more plot for his narrative. While respectful of David's story, which he has come by honestly over the course of his life, we respond out of the Christian story. We lift up God's abiding love as the cornerstone of the Christian story. We offer God's love as the foundational theme of David's story. God deeply loves David. God has not abandoned him. God was with Janet and him throughout their terrible ordeal. God is with David now in his suffering. God will move with him into a hopeful future. These concepts of God are new to David, and they therefore offer him more plot for his narrative. Where there is more plot, new interpretations and meanings are possible. Rather than feeling abandoned by God, David may come to believe that he has been held by God in the midst of his pain. Rather than struggling with meaninglessness, he may find ultimate meaning in God's love and bring a more yielding, trusting response to the mystery of life. Rather than feeling he has no future, he may come to trust that he can move with God into a hopeful, albeit still unclear, future.

Of course, such profound shifts of meaning take time. None of us can change overnight the deep sense we make of the world and our place in it. And the process of reconstructing meaning can be utterly draining. We seem to hear something of this expressed in the words of Frederick Buechner, reflecting after the death of his brother:

> I also want to get it right about whatever it is that is going on inside me now. There is the level of feeling where, after moments when the clouds seem to be lifting a little, it is suddenly all I can do to see the hand in front of my face. And there is the level of thinking, thinking back especially over our last few conversations, including the one within only three or four hours of his death when we said good-bye for good. But deeper down still there is a level that I know nothing about at all except that whatever I am doing there, it is absolutely exhausting. It is as if great quantities of furniture have to be moved from one place to another. There seem to be endless cartons of God only knows what to sort through somehow. The earth itself has to be bulldozed and shifted around and reshaped. A whole new landscape has to come into being.
> (1999, 147)

Given how painstaking and painful the reconstruction of meaning can be, the third thing a minister can offer David is consistent support as he struggles in this process. In chapter 3, I suggested that ministers can help people move over time toward greater security in attachment to God through consistency of care and consistency of message. The same is true in the realm of meaning-making. By consistently caring for his story and then placing it within the Christian story, we may help David ever so gradually shift his meaning system toward greater trust in God's love. The faith community also has a critical role to play in this regard. When we gather each week as a faith community, we are probably not aware that we are supporting grieving people in their reconstruction of meaning. Yet we are. Through its consistent presence and faithful witness to the Christian story, the faith community supports David as he expands his story, reinterprets his experience, and reconstructs meaning. This may be one of our greatest tasks and privileges.

The Mosaic of Grief

Every mosaic, like every work of art, tells a story. The mosaic of grief tells the story of one's losses and the meaning one has made of these losses. But stories and meanings can and do shift and change, as we have seen. Therefore, we might think of the mosaic of grief as a work always in progress. Not long ago I spoke with a man whose child died at birth almost thirty years ago. He said that he has recently begun to think about and make meaning of this sad loss in new and unexpected ways. Even now, thirty years later, his mosaic of grief is shifting and changing. A student in my grief and loss course once suggested that we think of the mosaic of grief as having cement that never fully dries, thus allowing for the ongoing emergence of new stories and new meanings over time. As we sort out our losses and their meanings, we may rearrange existing pieces, remove some pieces, or add new pieces to the mosaic. With these changes, the mosaic may take on different shadings and castings; new patterns may emerge, and the mosaic may tell a new story.

Ministers and faith communities have a critical role to play in this process as they care for stories, proffer God's love as the foundation of the Christian story, and offer consistent support for the hard work of meaning reconstruction after loss. Through all these means, we help others to revise their stories and reshape their meanings grounded in God's love. And what sustains us as we support others in this work? Perhaps most important, it is the conviction that we do not do this work alone. God is our partner in the reconstruction of meaning, "making all things new" (Rev. 21:5). Ultimately, making meaning after loss and moving with God into a hopeful future is less a task of grief than an experience of grace.

◆ ◆ ◆

Questions for Reflection

1. Everyone has a story. Spend some time reflecting on your story. What is the story of your life? What would you describe as the plotline of your story? Who are the major and minor characters in your story? Does your story have a primary theme or themes? How are past, present, and future connected in your story? Is your story sensible and coherent? What parts of your story have you learned and absorbed from your family, from your culture, from your faith tradition? What other sources have shaped your story, for better and/or for worse?

2. Our stories express the meaning of our lives. What is the meaning embedded in and expressed through your story? How does your story reflect how you understand the sense, purpose, and significance of your life? How does your story communicate what you value, what your priorities in life are, and what you believe? How does your story express how you understand yourself? How does your story reflect how you understand God's feelings about and responses to you?

3. When you have experienced loss, what has happened to your story and your meaning system? Have you ever experienced narrative disruption? Has your meaning system ever felt threatened? In your grief, have you been able eventually to affirm your meaning system? Have you ever faced the challenge of rewriting your

story and reconstructing your system of meaning? Have you ever felt the deep pain of meaninglessness?

4. Think about the concepts and understandings of God that have shaped your story and your meaning system. How would you describe your concept(s) of God? How do you understand and experience God when you are suffering? Does your story reflect the God of love who is with you always, even in the mystery of pain and suffering?

5. If David sought your help and support in the midst of his narrative disruption and threatened meaning, how might you respond to him, both initially and over time?

6. How might David's faith community respond to him in ways that could support him in his grief and in his reconstruction of meaning?

7. What questions or ideas flowing from this chapter might you want to bring to your prayer or to conversations with trusted friends or colleagues?

5

Grief, Stress, and Religious Coping

THE DISRUPTION OF one's narrative—of self and world—and the need to reconstruct meaning following loss are sources of great stress for many grieving people. Grief may cause other sorts of stress as well. When we experience stress, we typically try to relieve the pain of it by coping in particular ways. In this chapter, we will look at the topics of stress and coping and explore the place of religion in coping with grief.

Case Vignette

Angie is a thirty-six-year-old kindergarten teacher who is grieving the sudden death of her four-year-old son Tyler eleven months ago. From the time she was a little girl, Angie had had two dreams: to be a mother and to be a teacher. Angie's parents were unhappily married, and there was chronic tension and conflict between them. As the oldest of their three children, Angie felt responsible for trying to keep her parents together. She cooked and cleaned and did whatever else she could so that they would feel less stress. She also tried to protect her siblings from their parents' fighting. Angie felt that it was up to her to keep her family together, and this was a source of terrible pressure. She dreamed of the day she would be a mother and knew she would do whatever it took to create a happy family for herself.

Angie's family attended church together most Sundays. Angie often found this time warm and comforting. For at least this period of time, her parents weren't fighting. She liked the pastor very much. She enjoyed hearing about Jesus' love for little children, and loved the Bible story about Jesus gathering the little children to himself. One of Angie's Sunday school teachers gave her a picture of Jesus hugging little children. Sometimes when things were difficult at home, Angie would look at the picture and imagine Jesus hugging her. Angie also loved to sing the hymns at church. Her favorites were "His Eye Is on the Sparrow" and "He's Got the Whole World in His Hands." She tried to believe that God cares for everyone, even the little sparrows, and that God holds everyone in His hands, but sometimes it was hard. At home, she mostly felt that she was the one holding everything together.

Angie loved school. It was a haven for her from the stress at home, and she enjoyed learning. She decided at a young age to be a kindergarten teacher, and she planned for this future very carefully. She got a job after graduate school teaching kindergarten in a good school. Angie loved teaching. The children were terrific and so were her colleagues. She met Tom, a brother of one of her colleagues, after a few years of teaching. They had a sometimes rocky courtship but married after dating for two years.

Angie was eager to become a mother as soon as possible, but she had trouble conceiving. She sought out fertility specialists and underwent several months of grueling tests and procedures. Her joy was indescribable when she finally got pregnant and gave birth to a son. After Tyler was born, Angie's life revolved around being a mother, and she delighted in her new role. She was creating at last the happy family she had always dreamed of.

Angie and Tom belonged to a local faith community, which they liked very much. They did not attend worship regularly, but they planned to become more involved when Tyler got older. In the meantime Angie told Tyler stories about Jesus, and she taught him her favorite hymns from childhood.

One day when Tyler was four, he developed a fever and began vomiting. At first Angie and Tom were not overly concerned; they thought he might have a virus that was going around. But when Tyler suddenly lost consciousness, they frantically rushed him to the emergency room. He was diagnosed with meningitis. The emergency-room staff worked heroically to save Tyler, but he was pronounced dead about ten hours later. Angie and Tom, numb with shock, couldn't wrap their minds around what had happened. How could Tyler be dead, when just a day earlier he had been reciting his alphabet and playing with the dog in the backyard? The situation was surreal. Surely they were living in a horrendous nightmare.

Angie and Tom's pastor and members of their congregation came to the hospital and prayed with them the day Tyler died, and they came to be with them in their home in the days immediately following Tyler's death. Angie and Tom felt completely overwhelmed at the thought of planning a funeral for their son, so they were grateful when church members offered to plan it for them. The wake and the funeral were extraordinarily sad. The only thing that kept Tom and Angie going was the presence of so many caring people. At moments, Angie felt that the community was actually holding her up. The funeral was the hardest experience of her life. The most devastating moment was walking into church behind Tyler's small white casket. Angie later said, "No parents should ever have to walk behind their child's casket."

Angie felt numb for quite a long time after Tyler's death, and as the reality of her loss slowly seeped in, she felt like she had fallen into a bottomless pit of devastation. She felt her life irreparably shattered, and it was impossible for her to begin to imagine living without Tyler. Angie's life no longer made sense. Her dream of being a mother had been ripped away from her, with nothing to replace it. She also felt her life as a teacher slipping away because she felt unable to return to her job. Although Angie missed her students and her colleagues, she could not bear to see children who were just a little older than Tyler, and she could not bear thinking of Tyler never going to kindergarten.

Angie struggled in her relationships. She had a hard time being around even her closest friends. She only wanted to be with Tom and other people who knew what it meant to lose a child. Tom and Angie also began to have difficulties. They were grieving in different ways and didn't understand each other. Angie needed to talk about Tyler constantly. She was afraid of all the little details of his short life slipping away. Tom felt his heart ripped out with every mention of Tyler. He also felt overwhelmed by Angie's emotions and did not know how to comfort her. He buried himself in work, and Angie felt them drifting apart.

Daily encounters with others became a strain for Angie. She did not know how to answer when a new acquaintance asked her if she had children. Sometimes she would say no to spare herself the agony of recounting her son's death, but after doing so, Angie always felt enormous guilt, as if she had disowned Tyler. When she tried to describe Tyler's death, however, Angie would dissolve into tears in front of complete strangers. Some people urged them to have another child right away, but Angie and Tom knew that, even if they could conceive again, they could never replace Tyler. Angie was also terrified that something tragic could happen to a second child, and she did not think she could survive such devastating loss again.

In losing Tyler, Angie also lost her sense of self. She had been the one who always planned carefully and who held everything together, but she hadn't been able to protect her own son. She had failed in the most enormous way possible. No amount of hard work or detailed plans had kept Tyler alive. Everything she had lived for had slipped through her fingers. Angie felt overwhelmed and utterly broken, and she did not know how to hold all the brokenness. There were many days when she wondered how she would ever keep going.

In her anguish, Angie longed to feel her church community holding her up with their presence and prayers, as they had during the wake and funeral. But going to church was painful because it brought back memories of walking into the funeral behind Tyler's little white casket. Angie also longed to feel comfort from God. She had always tried to believe that God holds everyone in His hands, but now she felt completely abandoned. Angie was confused and angry. God was a parent. How could God not save Angie from the worst anguish a parent could endure? Jesus loved little children. How could Jesus not save Tyler? Why weren't God's eyes on Tyler, like they were on the sparrows in the hymn she loved so much? The Bible passages and hymns that used to offer comfort now seemed hollow, and Angie was disturbed by comments that people, thinking to comfort her, had made, such as, "God must have needed another angel in heaven," or "God never gives us more than we can handle." Were they suggesting that God had done this to Angie and Tom for some purpose? She was especially upset when someone said, "I wonder what lesson God is trying to teach you." Angie wanted desperately to reject this thought, but she began to worry that maybe God was trying to teach her something. She had not been as faithful in prayer and in church attendance in recent years. Was God punishing her for this? Had Tyler paid the price for her failings? Had God let them all fall through His hands?

Stress and Grief

Angie is enduring horrible pain and distress in virtually every part of her life: her marriage, her friendships, her work, her experience of church, and her relationship with God. Tyler's death shattered her story, her dreams for the future, and her very sense of self. Her life is in pieces, and she feels utterly broken. Angie's painful experience is not uncommon. Many people experience grief as a terrible sort of brokenness.[1] In order to respond to people in the brokenness of grief, we need to understand this experience more fully. One way to do so is to consider the brokenness of grief through the lens of *stress*. Grief often generates terrible stress in multiple domains. For example, grief may lead to terrible physical and psychiatric problems for some.

> There is no longer any doubt that the costs of bereavement in terms of health can be extreme. Bereaved individuals suffer elevated risks of depression, anxiety, and other psychiatric disorders, somatic complaints and infections, and a variety of other physical illnesses. They have higher consultation rates with doctors, use more medication, are hospitalized more often, and have more days of disability. The risk of mortality is associated with many different causes, including, particularly, suicide. (Stroebe, Hansson, Stroebe, & Schut 2001b, 8)

Grief may also cause emotional, cognitive, and interpersonal stress. After a significant loss, one's emotions may feel like a roller coaster swinging, dipping, surging. One may feel jolts of unfamiliar emotions, such as rage or despair. Or one may feel a disconcerting absence of emotion. One's thoughts may be completely jumbled, or one's mind may seem utterly empty. One's usual ways of thinking and understanding may be lost. As Ralph Waldo Emerson said, "Sorrow makes us all children again, destroys all differences of intellect. The wisest knows nothing" (Emerson & Forbes 1911, 153). In grief, one's relationships may suffer; a widow may no longer be included in "couples' evenings," or a teenager may not know how to talk to friends about his parents' divorce. For some people, grief may cause tremendous spiritual stress, posing a terrible challenge to their faith. Consider the powerful words of C. S. Lewis after the death of his beloved wife, Joy:

> Not that I am (I think) in much danger of ceasing to believe in God. The real danger is of coming to believe such dreadful things about Him. The conclusion I dread is not, "So there's no God after all," but, "So this is what God's really like. Deceive yourself no longer." (1961, 5)

Stress is a critical topic in a contemporary understanding of grief. Indeed, we cannot fully appreciate Angie's grief experience unless we understand the phenomenon of stress. What is stress, exactly? Susan Folkman, a researcher in stress and coping, has defined stress as "a relationship between the person and the environment that is appraised by the person as taxing or exceeding his or her resources and as endangering his or her well-being" (1984, 840). What does this mean? We are all in complex relationship with our environment. Our environment affects us, and we affect our environment. For example, the way power is exercised in my work environment may affect me significantly, for better and/or for worse. The ways I interact with colleagues may also affect my work environment significantly, for better and/or for worse. Sometimes the relationship between me and my environment may be challenging. For example, I may face the challenge of having limited time to complete a major project for school or work. When I face such a challenge, I typically muster all my available resources to respond to it. These resources may be internal, such as the ability to focus and block out distractions as well as a sense of confidence that I can do it. I may also draw on external resources such as asking friends or colleagues to help me.

Sometimes my available resources may not be adequate to meet the challenge, or at least I may not think they are adequate. For example, I may become anxious and distracted rather than focused when I think about the project I must complete. I may not believe I can succeed. Or my support system may not be available to help me at that moment. In such a case, I conclude that my available resources are not sufficient to manage the challenge I am facing. In the face of this discrepancy, what had been a potentially manageable challenge now becomes a *stressor*, and I experience *stress*.

For many people, there is no greater stressor than the
Everything about one's world is profoundly and irrepar...
one's resources—both internal and external—may be taxed beyond measure. This is the case with Angie. With Tyler's death, everything in her
life has fallen to pieces. She is struggling to hold her life together, and she
currently lacks sufficient internal and external resources to do so. She
is experiencing extreme stress. This is very worrisome because, as study
after study suggests, stress may be dangerous to one's health and well-
being. For instance, stress has been linked with Alzheimer's disease and
depression[2] as well as with fatigue, sleeplessness, irritability, and anger.[3]
Stress contributes to heart problems[4] and may also lead to interpersonal
difficulties,[5] while chronic stress may result in unhealthy weight increase[6]
and a shortened life span.[7]

What is the connection between stress and all of these possible outcomes? When we experience stress, our brains assume that we are facing
a significant threat and respond by releasing two hormones: adrenaline
and cortisol. In the short term, this "cascade of chemicals" (Carmichael
2009, 48) is helpful, as it girds our bodies for the "fight or flight" response;
that is, we will either do battle with our challenge or get the heck out
of there. When these chemicals are frequently present, however, they
may have damaging effects, such as those listed above. Over time they
also may adversely affect memory, learning, and the very structure of
the brain itself (Carmichael 2009). This is why chronic stress is so worrisome. With chronic stress comes a chronically activated stress response.
A study by researcher Anita DeLongis and colleagues suggests that the
"daily hassles" of life—that is, "the repeated or chronic strains of everyday life" (1982, 119) are more strongly and adversely related to physical health than major life events, perhaps because daily hassles keep the
stress hormones flowing. Stress can also create a dangerous ripple effect.
For instance, professors Rand Conger and M. Brent Donnellan (2007)
report that across many ethnicities, families who experience terrible financial hardship often experience many consequent stressors, such as marital
conflict and depression. Angie is experiencing terrible ripple effects of
Tyler's death in virtually every area of her life.

Clearly, stress can affect our bodies, our minds, and our lives in worrisome and even dangerous ways. However, it is critical to note that, while

some stress is part and parcel of life, there is great variability to it. People do not respond identically to the same situation. In some cases, one person's stressor is another person's stimulating challenge. And when people do experience stress, they are not affected in precisely the same ways; people negotiate stress in highly particular ways. Some degree of stress may even be beneficial, leading over time to strength and resilience. What accounts for such variability in the experience of and response to stress? The answer has to do with how we as individuals cope with the stressors in our lives.

Coping with Stress

Simply put, *coping* is our effort to manage stress. More formally, we can define coping as "the process through which individuals try to understand and deal with significant demands in their lives" (Ganzevoort 1998, 260, drawing on Pargament). There are a great many ways to cope. To sample this variety, let's go back to the example of having limited time to complete a major project. If this situation has become stressful, I may try to cope *cognitively*, such as by downplaying the importance of the project or telling myself that nothing is at stake if I miss the deadline. I may try to cope *behaviorally*, such as by asking for an extension of the deadline or by reducing the scope of the project. If my initial coping efforts don't succeed, I may go on to other cognitive and behavioral coping strategies. Some coping may be distinguished as either *emotion focused* or *problem focused* (VandenBos 2007, 232, 327, 735). In emotion-focused coping, my goal is to manage the negative emotional response I am having to a stressor rather than managing the stressor itself. So, for instance, in coping with my project, I may manage my anxiety and worry by talking with friends or going for a walk. In problem-focused coping, I deal with the stressor itself and work to reduce it or eliminate it. For example, I may work around the clock to be done with my project once and for all.

Along with the great range of ways to cope, there is also an array of possible outcomes of coping. Coping efforts are not always successful, and people may continue to experience stress. And some coping efforts may themselves lead to problems. For example, in a recent survey on stress in the United States conducted by the American Psychological Association, almost half of the 1,791 people surveyed reported eating poorly or overeating in an effort to manage stress; 18 percent reported managing stress through alcohol use (Martin 2008).

On the other hand, sometimes coping efforts are successful, and people experience a reduction or elimination of stress. And coping efforts may lead to another sort of positive outcome. Some people feel that, through their very efforts to cope with stress, they have not only managed their stress but also grown in positive and important ways. Researchers call this outcome *stress-related growth* (Park, Cohen, & Murch 1996) or *posttraumatic growth* (Calhoun & Tedeschi 2001). Let me quickly add that the presence of such growth does not mean people are grateful or glad that a stressor or trauma has happened. But when such an event does occur, many people describe feeling that they have grown in beneficial ways through their efforts to cope with it.

Some people feel that loss and grief pierce the "anesthetized state" (Vaughn 2003, 39) in which we sometimes go through life, and as a result people gain clarity about what is most important in life. The play Our Town, by Pulitzer-prize winning writer Thornton Wilder, offers a poignant expression of this growth in clarity. The play is set in Groveris Corners, New Hampshire at the turn of the twentieth century. It seems an ordinary small town in most ways. Adults work. Children go to school. Neighbors chat. The play features two families in particular, the Webbs and the Gibbs. We watch as young Emily Webb and George Gibbs grow up and enjoy a sweet courtship with each other. The second act closes with their wedding. In the third act, things take a more serious turn. It opens in the local cemetery, and we learn that nine years have gone by during which several townsfolk have died. Emily has died in childbirth, at the age of twenty-six. She is having trouble acclimating to being dead, and her mother-in-law, also now in the cemetery, encourages her to wait patiently until she begins to disconnect from the people and places she has loved. Emily does not want to do this. She wants to experience life again and begs the stage manager to allow her to go back and relive just one day in her life. Some in the cemetery warn her that this is a terrible idea, but Emily persists. She is granted her wish, and she chooses to go back and relive her twelfth birthday. At first, she is thrilled and delighted to see all the old familiar sights of Grover's Corners and her home. She is startled to realize how young her parents were at that time, and she wishes they could all stop and take in the preciousness of time spent together and of beautiful ordinary moments. But this doesn't happen, and the experience turns very bittersweet for Emily. She sees clearly that the living do not fully grasp the extraordinary gift of ordinary life. She asks to be taken back to the cemetery, but first she says a poignant farewell to all the ordinary and wonderful gifts of being alive.

People describe other sorts of stress-related growth too, such as stronger relationships with others, better coping skills, a deeper sense of spiritual or religious meaning in life, and an enhanced sense of self, perhaps derived in part from seeing what one is capable of enduring and managing when under stress.[8]

It's clear that there is great variability in coping, in terms of both what people try and the outcome of their efforts. What accounts for this variability? There are likely many factors at play, such as the nature and frequency of the stressor with which one is coping. For instance, a person may be able to muster sufficient resources to manage a onetime stressor, while chronic stress may wear down the person's coping capacities over time. Extreme stressors such as trauma may utterly overwhelm one's coping skills. Intense stress in childhood is always worrisome. Such stress, for which children have not yet developed sufficient coping skills, may interfere with proper neurological development and lead to a host of health problems in adulthood (Middlebrooks & Audage 2008). Social support is another critical variable in coping. Connections to supportive others seem to help with coping efforts and even buffer people from the effects of stress.[9]

Another factor that may underlie the variability in coping is what clinical psychologist and professor Kenneth Pargament (1997) calls our *orienting system*. According to Pargament, we do not experience crises or stress in a psychological vacuum. Rather, we all have a system of "well-established beliefs, practices, attitudes, goals, and values" (Pargament & Abu Raiya 2007, 743) that we bring to every situation and that shapes our response. This is our orienting system. When we experience stress, our orienting system shapes to some degree how we will try to cope; that is, "it makes some methods of coping more available to the individual than others" (Pargament 1997, 106). The orienting system contains both *resources* and *burdens*. For instance, my orienting system may include helpful resources, such as a belief that things usually work out. Such a belief may lead me to cope actively and optimistically with my problem. Conversely, my orienting system may include burdens that impede coping efforts, such as a lack of self-confidence. Such an attitude may make it hard for me to persist in coping, and I may be vulnerable to giving up.

But here is a critical point. While my particular orienting system may render some coping choices more available than others, my orienting system is not fixed and how I cope is not fated. There is always a moment when I must choose how specifically to cope with stress. There may come a time when I will choose to cope in a new way, trying something I have never done before. Such a choice may profoundly change the outcome of my coping. Furthermore, by coping in a new way, I may introduce something new to my orienting system, thereby expanding the coping repertoire I bring to future stressful moments (Pargament 1997). Psychiatrist Michael Miller (2008b) offers us an example. A familiar adage in twelve-step programs such as Alcoholics Anonymous is "Fake it till you make it." That is, people struggling with addiction are encouraged to follow the twelve-step tenets, even if they don't trust the program or themselves yet. We could say that they are being asked to cope in a new way, one that their orienting system may not yet support. The reasoning behind this adage is that behaving in a new way even before trust is present may in fact generate trust as people see that both they and the program can succeed. A research study of people struggling with cocaine addiction seems to confirm this idea (Crits-Christoph et al., 1999). Thus, coping is an active, constructive process, and change is always possible.

And one final point about the orienting system: it may itself be "vulnerable to stress" (McConnell et al. 2006, 1472). That is, any of us may reach a point in life where our orienting system succumbs to stress and no longer grounds or holds us in our efforts to cope. Two factors may shape whether or not we reach such a point: "the magnitude of the stressor and the strength of the orienting system" (ibid.). Thus, the orienting system, with its resources and its burdens, its strength and its vulnerability, plays an enormous role in our coping with stress.

Religious Coping

Angie is struggling mightily to cope with the death of her son. Sadly, her coping capacity is compromised in several ways. First, she is grieving the death of a child under traumatic circumstances. Under any circumstances, the death of a child may be a tremendous threat to a parent's well-being and sense of purpose and meaning. This may be exacerbated when the death is both sudden and unexpected. Such a traumatic loss may seriously undermine one's coping ability. Second, as she grieves this traumatic loss, Angie is disconnected from individuals and groups that could offer invaluable support; she is unable to work, thus losing the daily support of colleagues, and she is disconnected from close friends and from her faith community. Third, she and Tom are struggling in their relationship, in part because their ways of coping with their grief are markedly different. Angie's grieving is more *intuitive*, meaning it is centered in her emotional experience, while Tom's grieving style is more *instrumental*, meaning it is more cognitive and focused on problem solving (Martin & Doka 2000). Because they do not understand their different ways of grieving, their marriage is presently a source of disconnection and discord rather than empathy and mutual support.

Angie's orienting system, which contains her "well-established beliefs, practices, attitudes, goals, and values" (Pargament & Abu Raiya 2007, 743), is shaping her coping efforts. During her formative years, Angie coped with the stress and pain of her family life by being responsible, working hard, planning carefully for her own future, and believing she could create her dream of a happy family. These beliefs and practices became critical resources of her orienting system. But Tyler's death has made a mockery of them. What was the point of all her hard work and careful planning now that her dream of a happy family is dead? Angie's orienting system seems to contain no other resources at this time to ground her in her efforts to cope. She has no sense of God as present to her, comforting her and holding her. Even worse, in her efforts to understand Tyler's death, she is contemplating troubling ideas about God, such as whether Tyler's death constitutes a divine punishment for some infraction on her part. Ideas of God as abandoning or punishing are terrible burdens of the orienting system, and research shows clearly that these ideas can lead to very worrisome outcomes. In order to understand this critical aspect of Angie's experience, we turn to the area of *religious coping*.

I recently bought a calendar that offers a religious thought or exhortation for every day. The thought for one day was "I'm too blessed to be stressed." It seems the creators of this calendar saw a connection between stress and a particular religious belief, namely, that being blessed means an absence of stress. What is the connection, if any, between stress and religious beliefs?

Some people turn intentionally to various aspects of religion when faced with stress. That is, they engage in what researchers call *religious coping*. We know, of course, that religious coping has long been part of the human story. For thousands of years, religious people who have suffered loss have turned to their sacred scriptures as expressions of comfort, explanation, or lament. In recent years, the area of religious coping has become an important focus of social-scientific research, yielding critical and sometimes surprising results. The work of Kenneth Pargament, a researcher, clinician, and perhaps the world's foremost expert in the area of religious coping, is helpful in understanding why some people turn to religious coping in stressful times, what dimensions of religion they draw on, and what difference, if any, religious coping makes to people enduring stress.

Who Draws on Religious Coping?

Some say that "religion prospers in times of need" (Ganzevoort 1998, 260). While religious beliefs and behaviors may be important parts of one's daily life, these dimensions may become especially important at times of stress and crisis. For instance, immediately after the horrifying events of September 11, 2001, church attendance in the United States rose significantly (Goodstein 2001). Why might religion become especially important at such crisis moments? Religious philosopher John Smith (1968) proposes that times of crisis and transition, such as birth and death, contain something of the holy. The holiness of such transitions derives from two aspects. First, such moments bring us in touch with the essential ground and mystery of life. Second, they compel us to encounter our own limitations in the face of inexorable life forces. Religious ethicists David Little and Sumner Twiss (1973) use the term *boundary situations* to describe such times of crisis or transition when we face the limits of our own capacity to explain or resolve. In negotiating boundary situations, we may be especially likely to turn to religion, perhaps in large part because religion offers something beyond our own limits and the limits of this world (Pargament 1997; Wink & Dillon 2001). Importantly, though, while virtually everyone faces boundary situations in life, not everyone turns to religion in response. Pargament (1997) suggests that people are more likely to engage in religious coping if religion has been a consistent and compelling part of their lives and therefore of the orienting system that shapes their coping efforts. If religion has never been part of one's life or one has not found it important or compelling, it may not be a significant part of the orienting system that one brings to coping.

With Tyler's sudden death, Angie is facing the greatest boundary situation of her life, and she is unable to make sense of or manage it on her own. At times in her life, God and church community have been sources of great comfort for Angie. But at this time she is unable to access any comforting connection either to God or to her faith community; rather, she feels disconnected from her faith community, and she is drawing on some troubling ideas about God. These particular aspects do not bode well for Angie's coping and long-term well-being.

The Many Dimensions of Religious Coping

When people turn to religion as they cope with stress, to what exactly are they turning? Religion, of course, is a complex, multidimensional phenomenon, encompassing many varied aspects, such as "prayer, meditation, sacred literature, rituals, communal worship, tradition, reason, art, intimate human relationships, social compassion, and any number of other practices that have developed over the millennia" (Pargament 1997, 9, citing Streng 1976). People may draw on any or all of these dimensions when experiencing stress, and these dimensions may clearly overlap. While acknowledging the great complexity of religion, researchers in religious coping often focus on three primary dimensions: religious beliefs, religious practices, and religious community (Hummel 2003; Pargament 1997). Let's take a closer look at these aspects of religious coping, particularly as they may be manifest in times of stress and loss.

Religious Beliefs. In chapter 4, we saw how our beliefs help us to understand and make sense of our story and the story of the world. Our religious beliefs may become especially important in helping us to make sense of loss. For example, when a loved one dies, we may draw on religious beliefs to understand what follows death. In a research study I conducted on grief, many participants shared religious beliefs about what had become of their loved ones after death. Some expressed such hopeful beliefs as these: "She's in a better place," "He's at peace," "She's in heaven," "She's with the saints," "We believe we will be reunited with him again," and "She is happy with the Lord." People also engage religious beliefs about other aspects of loss, such as whether God is present or absent in suffering. We know that people often feel God's absence very painfully as they grieve.[10] C. S. Lewis described poignantly his sense of God's absence as he grieved for his wife:

> Meanwhile, where is God? This is one of the most disquieting symptoms. When you are happy, so happy that you have no sense of needing Him, so happy that you are tempted to feel His claims upon you as an interruption, if you remember yourself and turn to Him with gratitude and praise, you will be—or so it feels—welcomed with open arms. But go to Him when your need is desperate, when all other help is vain, and what do you find? A door slammed in your face, and a sound of bolting and double bolting on the inside. After that, silence. You may as well turn away. The longer you wait, the more emphatic the silence will become. There are no lights in the windows. It might be an empty house. Was it ever inhabited? It seemed so once. And that seeming was as strong as this. What can this mean? Why is He so present a commander in our time of prosperity and so very absent a help in time of trouble? (1961, 4–5)

In her grief, Angie is struggling in the realm of religious beliefs. Did God abandon Tyler? Has God abandoned Angie and Tom? Was Tyler's death some sort of divine punishment? She is not sure what to believe, and this is causing her great distress.

Religious Practice. A second dimension of religious coping is engaging in religious practices—such as prayer, hymn singing, worship, and ritual—in response to stress or loss. For example, the singing of spirituals and gospel songs has often been important to African Americans in times of struggle and suffering, such as in the dark days of slavery and more recently during the civil rights movement (Jason, Meier, & Jacobs 2009). Religious rituals, such as wake and funeral services and ongoing memorials for the dead, are important to many grieving people. Kerry Kennedy, daughter of Robert F. Kennedy, describes a significant religious ritual that she and her family observed each year after her father's death.

> Every May 29, we visited Uncle Jack's grave at Arlington National Cemetery, to remember his birthday, and then eight days later, on June 6, hundreds of old friends and family followed us home from Mass at Arlington, remembering my father's life. We'd each participate in the Mass, reading from scripture, taking up gifts, and singing 1960s folk songs and spirituals. Each reading was carefully chosen for its resonance of the issues Robert Kennedy devoted his life to: peace, justice, tolerance, courage, uplifting the poor, empowering citizens. (2008, xxvi)

In the past, Angie drew peace and comfort from certain hymns and prayers. For both Angie and Tom, the wake and funeral services for Tyler were very important religious rituals. But since the funeral, Angie has struggled to draw on any religious practices to help her in her grief. She has felt unable to pray, go to church, or sing the hymns that used to offer her comfort.

Religious Community. A third aspect of religious coping is connection to a religious or faith community in a time of crisis or loss. Members of a faith community may support grieving people in numerous ways, such as through their presence during wake and funeral services or through conversation, preparation of meals, annual memorial services, or bereavement support groups. Such support is enormously helpful to some grieving people. A participant in my research study shared how very significant were the prayers of her faith community before and after her husband's death:

> I'm a Baptist. I married a Baptist and that's how I became a Baptist and we were very committed to our church and our church work and I know that when W. got sick, those four days he was in the hospital, he was on the prayer line and people were praying that he would be well and when he died, it was like, didn't God hear what we were saying? But I really feel that those prayers, continued after his death, really . . . carried

me because I was so grief-stricken that I couldn't pray and . . . it was so critical for me at that time because I would start to pray and I would fall apart and it was like I couldn't make any sense out of it.

Sometimes people do not experience their faith community as supportive, or at least they do not know how to avail themselves of this support. This is the case with Angie. Her faith community was critically important at the time of Tyler's death. Some members of the community prayed with Angie and Tom and then helped to plan the funeral. Angie felt that the presence of the community at the wake and funeral held her up and carried her through. But since the funeral, Angie has struggled to connect with this community. She is having a hard time even walking into church, and she is not sure people understand her overwhelming anguish. She is struggling to connect with anyone except those who have also lost a child.

The Effects of Religious Coping

After the deaths of her parents, the singer-songwriter Rosanne Cash (2006) wrote, "I wish I was a Christian, and knew what to believe." Embedded in this lyric may be the assumption that religious beliefs provide comfort or clarity at a time of loss. Is this so? Are all religious coping efforts helpful to us at difficult times? While this is a complex domain, two decades of careful and nuanced research have made increasingly clear that all religious coping is not created equal.[11] In terms of effects on people's physical, mental, and spiritual well-being, some forms of religious coping seem beneficial while others appear to be downright harmful.

Some religious coping efforts seem to have helpful effects over time; in various research studies they are associated with feeling closer to one's church and to God,[12] with optimism in the face of racism,[13] with less depression,[14] with more stress-related growth over time,[15] and with better tolerance of chronic pain.[16] In contrast, other religious coping efforts seem to have worrisome effects over time; they are associated with greater depression and anxiety,[17] with greater sensitivity to physiological pain,[18] and even with increased risk of mortality.[19]

What can we say about the religious coping efforts that seem to help people in a stressful situation and to yield beneficial effects over time?

These efforts tend to have certain things in common. They "reflect a secure relationship with God, a belief that there is a greater meaning to be found, and a sense of spiritual connectedness with others" (Pargament & Abu Raiya 2007, 748). That is, when people believe that a loving, supportive God is with them in their struggles, that there is meaning in the midst of loss, and that they are spiritually connected to others as they struggle, they tend to cope well. Physically, mentally, and spiritually, they tend to do better over time.

What can we say about the religious coping efforts that do not seem to help people in a stressful situation but rather yield worrisome, harmful effects over time? These "spiritual risk factors" (Pargament & Saunders 2007, 904) tend to have certain things in common. They "reflect an ominous view of the world, and a religious struggle to find and conserve significance in life" (Pargament & Abu Raiya 2007, 748). That is, when people believe that the world is scary and threatening and when they struggle to hold on to a sense of significance in life, they tend not to cope as well. Physically, mentally, and spiritually, they tend to suffer over time.

For some people, an ominous view of the world seems to include the belief that, in a time of crisis or loss, they are being punished or abandoned by God. Consistently in research results, such belief seems to yield terrible outcomes. For example, the belief in a punishing God is associated with negative mood,[20] greater depression and anxiety among those whose children have died,[21] and increased sensitivity to pain.[22] An understanding of God as punishing and abandoning may even predict mortality. In a powerful study of 596 older hospital patients, Pargament and colleagues (2001) investigated how the patients understood their illness relative to their conception of God. Two years later, the researchers followed up with these patients. During those two years, 176 of them had died. The researchers did careful analytical comparisons of those who had died and those who were still alive. After controlling statistically for all the possible variables between these two groups in terms of physical health, mental health, and demographic variables (e.g., age, gender), a critical difference emerged. Those who had died were much more likely than those still alive to have felt that God had abandoned them and to doubt God's care and love for them.

Of course, any of us, in our humanity, may wonder at times if we are being punished or abandoned by God. Even Jesus seemed to articulate such struggle as he cried out, "My God, my God, why have you forsaken me?" (Matt. 27:46). While some people seem eventually to move through this struggle, however, others persist in understanding God as punishing or abandoning. Research suggests that these people may suffer worse outcomes over time (Pargament et al. 2004).[23]

We can now see clearly why Angie's religious coping efforts are cause for concern. First, she is not demonstrating any of the efforts that seem to yield helpful outcomes over time. That is, she is not experiencing a secure relationship with God. The meaning on which she has built her life has been shattered, with nothing yet to take its place. And she does not have a strong sense of spiritual connectedness with other people. Second, she is struggling in ways that tend to yield worrisome outcomes over time. She is wrestling with a view of the world as scary, and particularly of God as punishing and abandoning.

Given the tremendous stakes of religious coping efforts, this is an area we need to take very seriously. And it is also an area that cries out for even more precise study. For instance, some research suggests that there are important religious, ethnic, and cultural variations in religious coping efforts and outcomes.[24] We must continue to learn how religious coping influences the lives of grieving people, for better or for worse.

Religious Coping in Theological Perspective

Research results in religious coping are eye-opening and sometimes truly stunning. But, of course, research results never tell the whole story. How do we consider religious coping from a theological perspective? For many people, grief is an experience of terrible brokenness. Loss breaks our hearts and breaks our stories, perhaps leaving our lives in pieces. Our response to this brokenness is shaped by our orienting system, which is in large part what we have come to believe about the reality of life. From a Christian perspective, the core reality of life is God's love in Christ. "For God so loved the world that he gave his only Son, so that everyone who believes in him may not perish but may have eternal life" (John 3:16). God, who is "near to the brokenhearted" (Ps. 34:18) and "binds up their wounds" (Ps. 147:3), became flesh, in love. Jesus Christ, the bread of life broken for us, knows our brokenness and has promised to be with us always (Matt. 28:20). We are held always in our brokenness by God's love. When our coping efforts draw on this core reality, we will live with greater hope and trust. This holding doesn't undo our loss or unbreak our hearts. But while we may still grieve deeply, we believe we are loved, not punished. We believe we are held, not abandoned. God's love holds us in our brokenness. When we struggle with ideas of God as punishing or abandoning, we have lost touch with the core reality of God's love and are instead drawing on a distortion of reality. This distortion cannot hold us in our brokenness, and we are left feeling fragmented and forsaken.

And as God's love holds us in our brokenness, so we are called to hold each other in the brokenness of grief. We might imagine that, from the cross, Jesus saw the grief of both his mother and his disciple, and he called them to hold each other. "When Jesus saw his mother and the disciple whom he loved standing beside her, he said to his mother, 'Woman, here is your son.' Then he said to the disciple, 'Here is your mother.' And from that hour the disciple took her into his own home" (John 19:26-27). Brokenness is part of life. While each experience of brokenness is particular, a human thread runs through them all. Holding each other in our brokenness is our response to our shared humanity and to our Christian call.

Religious Coping, Attachment, and Meaning-Making

Why do some people draw on helpful religious coping—that is, a secure relationship with God and a sense of meaning in their loss—while others struggle with harmful religious coping—that is, a sense of the world as scary and of God as punishing and abandoning? Importantly, these questions bring us back around to the topics of attachment to God and meaning-making after loss. Our particular religious coping efforts reflect our God concept and our sense of meaning. With a secure attachment to God, we may have a fundamental sense of trust, security, and safety, even in the midst of loss. This is a foundational part of the orienting system we bring to our coping. When we are oriented to this reality, we feel tethered in an ultimate sense to a loving, cherishing God who holds us in our brokenness, and our coping efforts will help us to feel that life has meaning, even in the brokenness, because God's love holds it all.

With an insecure attachment to God, we may have a fundamental sense of anxiety and fear that is heightened in a time of loss. This is a foundational part of the orienting system we bring to our coping. As we struggle with loss, we may understand the world as scary and threatening, and we may experience God as inconsistent, abandoning, and even punishing. When we are oriented to this distortion of reality, we may not feel held by love. We may struggle mightily in our search for significance after loss, and we may feel utterly forsaken.

Ministerial Perspective

From a ministerial perspective, what sort of care and companioning might be most helpful to Angie in her great pain? First, *a minister can attend to Angie's religious beliefs*. In her grief, Angie is struggling with the terrible question of whether Tyler's death is punishment from God for some infraction on her part. She feels abandoned by God in the midst of her sorrow. She does not feel held in the brokenness of grief. These beliefs represent a terrible distortion of the heart of reality, which is that God's love holds us in the brokenness of grief. Therefore, with sensitivity, we want to counter these ideas consistently and compassionately. According to a Hasidic story, a rabbi told his people to study the Torah so that they would have Scripture on their hearts. "One of them asked, 'Why *on* our hearts, and not *in* them?' The rabbi answered, 'Only God can put Scripture inside. But reading sacred text can put it on your hearts, and then when your hearts break, the holy words will fall inside'" (Lamott 2005, 73). In our preaching, teaching, and pastoral care, we want to articulate God's love and care again and again, so that the words are there to fall inside when people's hearts break.

Second, *a minister can attend to Angie's religious practices*. In the past, certain Bible passages, pictures, and hymns were very important to Angie and helped her to feel God as lovingly present to her. An important piece of pastoral work with Angie might be to help her reconnect with these. For example, certain hymns were soothing to Angie when she was young. She also taught these hymns to Tyler. With time, Angie may be able to reclaim these hymns, letting the words and music hold her again as they once did. They might also be a way of continuing to feel an important connection to Tyler. Likewise, the Scripture passages of Jesus welcoming the little children (Matt. 19:13-15; Mark 10:13-16; Luke 18:15-17) were once a great comfort to Angie. In returning to these passages, she might be able to imagine Jesus gathering Tyler to himself and holding him. This may relieve her of her terrible sense of failure that she let Tyler slip through her hands. She might also be able to imagine Jesus gathering her to himself. The same God who loved her as a child loves her still and holds her in her brokenness.

Also, we might encourage Angie to pray in some new ways. For example, these beautiful words of 1 John may speak to her powerfully in her present struggle: "*God is love*, and those who abide in love abide in God, and God abides in them. Love has been perfected among us in this: that we may have boldness on the day of judgment, because as he is, so are we in this world. *There is no fear in love*, but perfect love casts out fear; for *fear has to do with punishment*, and whoever fears has not reached perfection in love. We love because *he first loved us*" (1 John 4:16–19, emphasis added). Over time, these words might fall into Angie's broken heart, helping her to feel loved and held in her sorrow.

Third, *a minister can sensitively encourage Angie to reconnect with her faith community*. As the research on religious coping makes clear, members of the faith community are not incidental to each other's well-being. One's faith community plays a potentially enormous role in one's coping with loss. In a Christian context, the faith community comes together to recall the story of God's love incarnated in Jesus Christ. And we try, however imperfectly, to incarnate this love for one another, especially by holding one another in times of suffering and struggle. Frederick Buechner tells the story of waiting for an elevator when he was young. When the elevator doors opened, he saw Franklin Delano Roosevelt, who was then paralyzed, being held up by two men. Buechner says, "What I learned for the first time from that glimpse I had of him in the elevator is that even the mightiest among us can't stand on our own. Unless we have someone to hold us, our flimsy legs buckle" (2008, 21). So it is with each of us. When sorrow strikes, our flimsy legs may well buckle, and we need others to hold us up. We often come to feel held by God precisely through the way that we are held by others.

Angie's faith community has already been a great support to her in her grief. Members of her community prayed with Angie and Tom in the hospital. Some then planned the funeral service. During the wake and funeral, it was the sense of being held up by so many caring people that allowed Angie to get through the horrific ordeal. There are many other ways in which Angie's faith community can continue to support her in her grief. Individuals can send cards or make phone calls. A bereavement support group in the parish can welcome Angie and Tom to join them as they feel able.[25] A bereavement ministry team can invite them to special services of remembrance for those who have died. Such a group can also anticipate the great pain of days like Christmas, Mother's Day, and Father's Day for those who have lost children; they can write special prayers or light a memorial candle in honor of these children. The faith community may be able to help Angie in some other very personal ways. For instance, Angie is having trouble coming back to church because it is such a painful reminder of Tyler's funeral. Angie may be deeply touched by someone's offer to walk into church with her and sit beside her. Angie cannot yet sing her old favorite hymns. But the community can, and this may be deeply moving to Angie. All of these efforts may help her to feel held by the community. And as she is held by the faith community, so she is held by God. She has not fallen through God's hands.

The Mosaic of Grief

Mosaics emerge from brokenness. They are made of pieces, fragments, and shards; they are marked by spaces, gaps, and cracks. The mosaic of grief also emerges from brokenness. After loss, our lives may feel shattered and in pieces, and we may feel we are alone with our brokenness and suffering. But we are not alone. God's love, the heart of reality, holds us in the brokenness of grief. Ministers and faith communities play a critical role in communicating and incarnating this love. The lyrics to Leonard Cohen's song "Anthem" (1992) help us to understand something of this role:

> Ring the bells that still can ring.
> Forget your perfect offering.
> There is a crack in everything.
> That's how the light gets in.

We cannot protect each other from the brokenness of grief, nor can we put the pieces back together just so. There is a crack in everything. But through our care, through our prayer, and through our faithful presence, we hold each other in our brokenness. And just so, the light of God gets in.

◆   ◆   ◆

Questions for Reflection

1. Stress is part of life. Spend some time reflecting on the stress that you have had to manage in your life. What were the stressors of your childhood? What have been the stressors of adulthood? What stress have you experienced in times of loss and grief?

2. At this point in your life, how do you typically cope with stress? Are your coping efforts usually successful—that is, do you experience less stress? Are they ever unsuccessful? Have your methods of coping changed at all over time? How might your style of coping with stress influence your ways of ministering to others?

3. As part of coping with stress or loss, do you draw on any particular religious beliefs, religious practices, or other aspects of religion? Think about the understandings of God that you draw on in a time of need. Do you draw on the God of love who holds you in your brokenness? Do you ever struggle with the fear that God may be punishing you or abandoning you in your time of suffering? If so, can you recall and reconnect to graced moments in your life when you have felt held by the God of love?

4. As part of coping with stress or loss, do you ever turn to a faith community to support you? If so, what has this experience been like for you? Have you felt held by the faith community in your experience of brokenness? Has the faith community been a means of your coming to feel held by the God of love?

5. Think of grieving people to whom you have ministered or are ministering now. How might an understanding of religious coping shed light on some of their struggles? How might this

understanding shape or inform your ways of ministering to them?

6. If Angie sought your help and support in the midst of her terrible grief and religious struggles, how might you respond to her, both initially and over time? How might Angie's faith community respond to her in ways that could support her in her grief and help her to feel held by God and by others in her brokenness?

7. What questions or ideas flowing from this chapter might you want to bring to your prayer or to conversations with trusted friends or colleagues?

6

Grief in Relational Perspective

ONE OF THE critiques of traditional grief theory is that it understands grief as a largely individual and intrapsychic process; that is, grief is a private affair, and one grieves primarily within oneself and by oneself. In contrast, some contemporary grief theory recognizes that grief is a profoundly relational experience, and it emphasizes the important ways in which this is so. Beginning with a case vignette, in this chapter we look more fully at grief in relational perspective.

Case Vignette

Barry is a forty-six-year-old technology consultant who is grieving the death of his close friend Ed ten months ago. Barry grew up an only child in a small community in the northeastern United States. Barry's parents were both born during the Depression, and their early years were marked by great deprivation and struggle. Barry's maternal grandfather abandoned his family soon after Barry's mother, Bernice, was born, leaving her family literally penniless and often going hungry. As a girl, Bernice found some comfort in books and dreamed of someday becoming a librarian. But her mother told her this was impossible and she needed to "think small" about her life. Bernice quit school in the tenth grade to help support her family. Barry's father, Charles, was the oldest of four children. His youngest sister was born with a congenital heart defect and died before her first birthday. Charles's parents never recovered from her death and spent the rest of their lives in a largely depressed state, emotionally disconnected from their other children.

During childhood, Barry's home life was stable and predictable. He liked school and loved sports, especially Little League baseball, which he played for several years. He had many buddies. And yet a bleakness permeated his family. Due to their painful histories, Barry's parents had a grim outlook on life, and they saw life as something to be endured rather than enjoyed. Barry's father worried a lot about something terrible happening to Barry, as it did to his youngest sister. Barry's mother was afraid of Barry having his hopes for his future dashed, as hers were, and so she frequently encouraged him to "think small" about his life. For instance, he enjoyed painting and drawing and dreamed that someday he could be an artist. His mother discouraged this and encouraged him to think practically instead. The family belonged to the local church, but they weren't very involved. Barry occasionally asked his parents about God and religion. Neither of them experienced God as a faithful, loving presence in their lives. Barry's own experience of God was of a fairly distant and unfeeling being; he wanted to believe in a loving God but did not really know how.

During junior high school, Barry gradually began to sense that he was different in an important way from his friends. He was not preoccupied, as they increasingly were, with the girls at school, and this confused him. Why didn't he care about the girls? Why didn't he want to flirt with them? Barry was afraid of being made fun of if he shared this with his friends, so for a long time he simply pretended that he, too, cared about girls. But he grew worried and scared. What was wrong with him? In the tenth grade, Barry had a wonderful history teacher who was both smart and kind. He finally worked up the nerve to talk with Mrs. Rhynne after class about his worry. She was very supportive. She told Barry that it was okay not to like girls. She said he would continue to learn more about himself as he got older and for now needed to be patient with himself. Over the next couple of years, Barry talked many times with Mrs. Rhynne, and with another supportive teacher. What he gradually came to know was that he was drawn in a fundamental way to boys rather than to girls. He didn't really understand this, but he knew deep within that it was so. He was grateful to his teachers who supported him. But he also heard his friends and other people talk in horrible ways about homosexuals. His friends jokingly insulted each other with terms like "fag" and "queer." It became horrifyingly clear to Barry that his life could change dramatically for the worse if he shared this deep truth about himself. He also did not know how his parents would respond to him. He kept his secret mostly to himself and felt increasingly lonely.

Finally, as he approached his high school graduation, Barry mustered the courage to tell his parents that he was gay. They were shocked. At first they responded with some supportive words. But over the next few days and weeks, he received a different reaction. Both of them seemed to become depressed about Barry's life. They said that people would be cruel and hostile to him, and they predicted nothing but sadness and loneliness for him if he continued on this path. They seemed to have no hope that he could ever be happy in life. Barry felt like he was suffocating in the gloom and doom.

After an excruciating summer at home, Barry could not wait to get to college. He hoped and dreamed that he would find a good group of friends and could be happy and enjoy life. Thankfully, this began to happen in his second year. Although he heard lots of gay jokes and antigay comments around campus, he made some wonderful friends through classes and other activities. By the end of his sophomore year, he had three very close friends, all of whom were gay: Adam, Sam, and Ed. The four of them were inseparable. They did everything together, and they had countless late-night discussions about everything from the best pizza in the city to the meaning of life. Sometimes they fought, too, but through it all Barry felt his life opening up in hopeful and exciting ways. He was learning about himself and becoming the person he was meant to be. Life seemed full of possibilities. He was certain that these people would be his closest friends for the rest of his life.

After graduation, they did stay close, sharing an apartment for two years. Then when Adam and Sam moved to other parts of the country for work, they still talked frequently on the phone and got together three or four times a year. Heeding his mother's advice to do something practical, Barry pursued a career in computer technology, with some success, and he made other close friendships. Despite these good things, his parents continued to bemoan the loneliness and sadness he would know as a gay man. Sometimes when he encountered homophobia and even outright hostility toward homosexuals, he started to worry that they could be right, but then he thought about Adam, Sam, and Ed. With his best friends, he was going to have a happy, full life and prove his parents wrong.

At their fifth college reunion, Sam didn't look good. After a lot of prodding from his friends, he finally saw a doctor a few weeks later. They were stunned to learn that he had AIDS, the terrifying disease for which there was no cure. Sam was going to die, and there was nothing they could do to stop it. Barry felt his heart break into a million pieces. He could not bear to think of Sam dying so young. It was intolerable to think of all that Sam would never experience, all that he would never contribute to the world because of this tragic illness. And he couldn't begin to imagine the rest of them going on without Sam. As if things weren't already unbearable, the growing AIDS epidemic had become a lightning rod in the country, with many voices insisting that AIDS was a punishment from God for immoral behavior. Even Barry's parents sometimes wondered if this was the case. At a time when Barry just wanted to be present to Sam, he found himself preoccupied by the judgments swirling around them. Sam's family was mostly invisible during his whole illness. They didn't understand homosexuality and felt that Sam had brought shame upon the family. Barry, Ed, and Adam became Sam's family. They arranged their lives so that one of them was with Sam as much as possible. All three of them were there when Sam died almost two years later. When it came time for the services, though, Sam's family took over and barely acknowledged Sam's closest friends.

Barry was certain his heart would never heal, and he hoped and prayed that nothing else would touch the small circle of Ed, Adam, and himself. It was a surreal nightmare when, a year later, Adam shared the horrific news that he, too, had AIDS. Barry felt like he was living in a slow-moving dream, unable to take in the reality. It just wasn't possible that Adam, too, was going to die. This was some sort of cruel cosmic joke. And yet he watched Adam get weaker and weaker. Barry and Ed were with Adam when he died eighteen months later. Two of the closest friends Barry had ever had were gone. The grief was unbearable. Barry began to think perhaps his parents were right and that life really was something to be endured rather than enjoyed. He struggled to feel hope that life could still hold good things for him.

Through their shared grief, Barry and Ed became closer than ever. Ed was like the brother Barry had always wished for. Over the next few years, they saw each other through all the ups and downs of careers, family, and relationships. They also talked a lot about Adam and Sam, trying to make sense of their deaths. Sometimes they talked about whether their deaths, as well as the countless other deaths from AIDS, could be a punishment from God. Ed, who had had experiences of feeling deeply loved by God in his life, was certain that they were not. Barry wasn't so sure. He still experienced God as a largely remote and unfeeling figure. Through his conversations with Ed, though, he began to hope that he, too, could feel loved by God. He had visited a few churches in the past but had not felt comfortable. One church had been downright cruel, leaving him feeling shamed and deficient by virtue of being gay. One weekend he joined Ed at his church. It was a wonderful experience. It was the first time he felt really comfortable and accepted in a church. Slowly, this became Barry's church community too.

Very gradually, Barry began to feel hopeful about life again. As effective AIDS treatments finally became available, he watched fewer people die painful deaths. He developed his career and enjoyed some wonderful friendships. With Ed's encouragement, he began to do some painting on the side and rediscovered his love for art. He also entered into a promising partnership with Michael, whom he met through work. Ed was their biggest supporter. Barry began to trust that, despite so much loss and sadness, he did not have to think small about life but instead could be happy and hopeful. But when he was forty-five, Barry got a call that shook all of this to the core. Ed had been diagnosed with an aggressive cancer. Barry felt the old surreal nightmare descend on him again. How could this possibly be? He and Ed had already lost so much. And why Ed? He was such a good person and believed in a loving God. Almost automatically, Barry began to do the things he knew he needed to do. He spent as much time as possible with Ed until his death fourteen months later.

Barry was devastated. Although many people were sympathetic that he had lost a close friend, no one seemed to understand the enormity of this loss. They were the last survivors of the circle of friends that had once meant everything to Barry. Only Ed had fully understood the loss of Adam and Sam. And it was mostly because of Ed that Barry had begun to rebuild hope for his life and seek a closer relationship with God. Now Ed was gone. The hope that Barry had painstakingly built felt dashed. Maybe his parents were right after all; maybe he should think small about life. Maybe life was mostly to be endured rather than enjoyed.

A Relational Perspective on Grief

Barry has suffered tremendous loss. His three closest friends have died. It was with these friends that Barry first began to think about his life in hopeful, expansive ways. It was through Ed that Barry began to hope that he could come to know a loving God. The deaths of his friends have shaken his hope profoundly, and he does not know how to think about his life or about his relationship with God. Barry has lost the most important relationships of his life and is struggling to feel any hope as he grieves.

As we see clearly with Barry, grief is a profoundly relational experience. Such an assertion may seem overstated or even wrong, at least initially. Many people have been taught by family or culture to think of grief as very private and as something best managed by oneself. But regardless of our outward expression of grief, or lack thereof, it is still a relational experience. How is this so? I would like to consider four aspects of grief in relational perspective.

First, we are, at our core, relational beings. While we might sometimes think of ourselves as independent and autonomous, we're not. Virtually everything about us as individuals is shaped and influenced by our relationships. We see this clearly with attachment theory. Infants in relationship with consistent and responsive caregivers tend to develop a secure attachment style; infants in relationship with inconsistent or unresponsive caregivers tend to develop an insecure attachment style. The attachment style formed in one's earliest days tends to have significant effects on one's other relationships throughout the life span.[1] In the last two decades, important research from the Stone Center at Wellesley College has also helped us to understand that we are "selves-in-relation," and our development as individuals is profoundly and inextricably linked to our relationships with others, for better or for worse (Jordan et al. 1991). This is the case with Barry. His relationships with his parents have been stultifying in painful ways, teaching him to think small about himself and to see life as a grim enterprise, mostly to be endured. In contrast, the relationships he enjoyed with Adam, Sam, and Ed helped him to develop, define, and value himself in expansive and life-giving ways. They also helped him to know hope for life where before he had known bleakness and gloom.

Because of "the gift of relationality at the very center of what it means to be human" (Howe 1995, 69), loss of significant people in our lives may cut to our core, leaving us feeling as if a part of our very selves has been destroyed. This is what has happened to Barry. The deaths of his three closest friends have left a devastating hole in his heart and in his life. It is as if a part of himself has also died. Importantly, we are in relationship to more than people. We may be in relationship throughout our lives to groups, to communities, to beliefs, to causes, to dreams, to religions, and to God. When any relationship in which we have been deeply invested is disrupted or destroyed by loss, we will likely grieve because, as psychiatrist Colin Murray Parkes suggests, grief is "the cost of commitment" (1996, 6).

Thus, as relational beings, we are always vulnerable to grief. And when we grieve, our experience of grief is further shaped by our relationships. This is the second aspect of grief in relational perspective. We may feel very supported by our family, friends, and colleagues as we grieve, and this may help us to endure our pain. On the other hand, some people find that they are isolated in their grief, at least initially, and this may augment their pain. For instance, widowed people sometimes find that they are no longer included in plans involving other couples, and divorced people sometimes feel they have been "dropped" by friends more sympathetic to their former spouse. When Sam died, his family largely ignored Barry, Adam, and Ed. They were marginalized, and their grief was disenfranchised.[2] In grieving for Ed, Barry is struggling to find relationships of support. Sometimes people don't understand the potential enormity of losing a friend, and adequate support is not forthcoming.

This brings us to the third aspect of grief in relational perspective. According to an African saying, "If you want to go fast, walk alone. But if you want to go far, walk with others." Grief is often a long and sometimes arduous journey, best negotiated with companionship and support. We need others as we grieve. And a critical way in which we need others is in revising our story and making meaning after loss. In chapter 4, we saw that when our life story and meaning system are disrupted or even destroyed by loss, we face the sometimes terrible challenge of creating a new narrative and reconstructing meaning. But we cannot do this alone. In *Four Quartets*, the poet T. S. Eliot wrote, "We had the experience but missed the meaning" (1971, 133). We need others to hear our stories and help us sort out the meanings. Our stories and our meanings are always co-constructed by others (Neimeyer 1999, 2001a, 2001d). As Barry grieved the deaths of Adam and Sam, Ed helped him to wrestle with meaning, including whether AIDS was a punishment from God and whether life still offered good things. As he now grieves the death of Ed, Barry needs relationships of support to help him make meaning again and create a hopeful, expansive narrative for his future.

Thus, our experience of grief is significantly shaped by our relationships. In ways that may be harder to notice, our experience of grief will also affect and perhaps change our relationships. This is the fourth aspect of grief in relational perspective. For instance, there is something about the experience of grief that sometimes connects people in ways that nothing else can. Eleanor Roosevelt expressed this in a letter to her husband, Franklin, when she was with relatives after a devastating loss. " 'It is a curious thing in human experience,' she said, 'people can be happy together and look back on their contacts very pleasantly, but such contacts will not make the same kind of bond that sorrow lived through together will create'" (Persico 2008, 134–35). This was certainly the case with Barry and Ed as they grieved the deaths of Adam and Sam. Their shared grief forged an even deeper bond between them and helped them to find healing. Even when such a deep bond does not result, grief will still affect our relationships. Loss changes us, in ways both dramatic and subtle. There is no returning to what life was like before the loss. We have to live into the "new normal" that will eventually emerge. When we are changed, our relationships also change. We bring a different self to our relationships, our friendships, our work, our ministry. The person with whom everyone in our life interacts is now different, if only slightly so, so that all of these relationships must shift, if only slightly so. Thus, to greater or lesser degrees, everyone in relationship with us must also discover their "new normal."

Theological Perspective

As he faces his "new normal," Barry is struggling mightily in the realm of hope. This is the case for many grieving people. Grief can devastate our hope about what is possible in life and what God intends for us. Because we are relational people, we often turn to our human relationships to offer hope that our story isn't over and that there is more to life than pain and sadness. But all human relationships—even the best of them—are limited. Barry's parents, because of their life experiences, could not communicate hope to him. Rather, they encouraged him to see the world as bleak and burdensome and to think small about his life. Ed was Barry's greatest source of hope, but this lifeline was lost with his death. No human being can fully provide the ultimate secure base on which to build a hopeful life. Ultimate security and ultimate hope come only through God, "an abiding Presence that sustains us even in the midst of things that are passing away" (Bennett 1997, 31).

How can we understand God as the source of ultimate hope after loss? We begin by recalling that the heart of the Christian faith is Emmanuel: God with us. Our God is a relational God, always present to us and, as St. Augustine believed, nearer to us than we are to ourselves. This God is not distant or detached. Even when we cannot sense God's presence, God is with us. Above the door of his house in Zurich, the psychiatrist Carl Jung had inscribed the words *Vocatus atque non vocatus, Deus aderit*, which in translation mean "Whether called or not, God will be present" (Bair 2003, 126). So it is. We are in relationship always to a faithful, relational God. God has been present to Barry throughout his life. When his parents communicated a distant, detached God, God was present. When his friends suffered and died, God was present. As Barry struggles to find hope, God is present.

But simply knowing God is present does not necessarily generate hope. For instance, if one is in relationship with a frightening or punishing God, knowing that this God is present could create fear or dread, rather than hope. Václav Havel, the playwright and former president of Czechoslovakia, has said, "Hope . . . is not the conviction that something will turn out well, but the certainty that something makes sense, regardless of how it turns out" (1990, 181). For Christians, the deep sense that generates hope in grief flows from the certainty that God is love, and abundantly so. God loves us "with an everlasting love" (Jer. 31:3), made manifest for all time in the life, death, and resurrection of Jesus the Christ. As Paul tells us, nothing can separate us from the love of God in Christ (Rom. 8:35-39).

Wholeness from the Brokenness of Grief

Let us consider more closely how the love of God is the source of hope in our grief. In the last chapter, we saw that when we grieve, we may feel that our lives are broken and fragmented. Everything is in pieces—our hearts, our stories, our relationships, our hopes. I proposed that God holds us in the brokenness of grief. Now I will add that God does more than hold us in our brokenness. God's love is active and creative. In love, God is constantly at work, restoring and renewing, bringing forth a new creation in Christ. The brokenness of grief is never the end of the story, nor is it the full story. Through God's love, a fundamental integrity or wholeness may emerge from all of the pieces. That is, in love, God seeks to bring *wholeness* out of the brokenness of grief.

What is the wholeness that may emerge from the brokenness of grief, through God's love? I would like to suggest three dimensions of this wholeness. First, sometimes through our grief we see things about ourselves, others, the world, and God that perhaps we would not see in any other way; that is, we come to see life in fuller, *more whole* ways. Sometimes what we see is terrible. We see suffering. We see injustice. We see cruelty and evil. We see our own capacity for all of these things. But we see other things, too. As we are broken by grief, we may break through to new insights and deeper clarity about faith, life, love, and loss.[3] We learn what really matters in life. We clarify the meanings by which we want to order our lives. And in this process, we may come deeply to know God's loving presence in our very suffering. Theologian S. Bruce Vaughn described such a powerful experience after the death of his young son:

> Grief, if we allow it to appropriately devastate us, breaks the hold that the mesmerizing everydayness of our world has upon our souls. It makes us aware of that deeper reality from which we live and move and have our being. It is only in this sense, it seems to me, that we can speak of God as being present to us. It is a presence that, as in grief, comes not instead of or in spite of absence, but through and by means of absence. Nevertheless, this divine presence is sufficient to ground our hope that love is eternal, that our fundamental longings and attachments are not futile. This hopeful faith, this faithful hope, enables us to love even though we know this very love will bring us to devastating loss. And it enables us to

enjoy the beauty of this life, despite the knowledge that the objects of
our joy will fade and pass away. Otherwise we inevitably draw back from
the edge of the abyss, and in doing so lose our own souls. (2003, 42)

A second part of the wholeness that may emerge from the brokenness of grief, through God's love, is recognizing how deeply connected
we all are. Because each experience of grief is particular, there is a certain "solitude of suffering" (Wolterstorff 1987, 25). And yet, as we endure
our own brokenness, we come to understand more deeply and fully that
brokenness is part of life. In our brokenness, we are connected to every
person who has ever grieved and who ever will grieve. There is always
someone on "humanity's mourning bench" (ibid., 63). In his suffering,
Barry is linked to all those who have ever suffered. In its great particularity, his grief is also a part of the *whole* of humanity. We are never alone.
Grief connects us all.

As paradoxical and perhaps absurd as it may sound, a third part of
the wholeness that may emerge from the brokenness of grief, through
God's love, is seeing abundance even amid our suffering. In the Gospel of
John, we hear Jesus' words, "I came that they may have life, and have it
abundantly" (John 10:10). Abundance is part of the *wholeness* that defines
life in Christ. We are always surrounded by God's abundance in countless
ways: the stunning fecundity of the natural world, the kindness of strangers, the compassion of friends. While God's abundance is always present,
it is sometimes in our grief that we are most open to and surprised by
it. At a time in my life when I was grieving some painful losses, I made
an eight-day silent retreat at the ocean. As I prayed, slowly walked the
beach, and talked with my spiritual director, I was astonished over and
over by the abundance I encountered. God continued to surprise me and,
indeed, take my breath away with gifts of comfort, beauty, clarity, and
hope. While I was still in much pain, I felt surrounded and held by God's
abundance. I knew on a deeply visceral level that God's abundance was
bigger than my grief, and this gave me great hope. I knew that good things
awaited me, my deep pain notwithstanding.

Of course, the idea of abundance may seem absolutely bizarre to us,
especially at a time of suffering. But God is always in relationship to us
in abundantly loving ways. And a part of God's abundant love is God's

inviting us in our grief to move toward a hopeful future. Sometimes, as was the case with Barry, people are encouraged to think small about their lives and their futures. They are discouraged from imagining their lives in hopeful, expansive ways. And after loss they may struggle to imagine a future for themselves at all. Professor and pastoral counselor Andrew Lester suggests that the inability to imagine a future for oneself is the greatest impediment to hope. Indeed, if we cannot imagine a future for ourselves, in what exactly would we have hope? But in love, God is "out in front of us calling us into an open-ended future" (Lester 1995, 2). A part of the wholeness that may emerge from the brokenness of grief is learning that "a new future is always available to us, that numerous possibilities exist in every present circumstance" (ibid.). Of course, hope must be tempered with an understanding of reality. It is not the case that anything is possible at any time in one's life. But it is the case that, through God's love, "in every end a new beginning lies hidden" (Moltmann 2004, 35), and God beckons us toward this new and hopeful beginning.

Thus, wholeness may emerge from the brokenness of grief. We may come to see ourselves, others, and life in fuller, more whole ways. We may come to realize how deeply connected we all are. We may come to know that God's abundant love surrounds us and beckons us beyond our grief, into a hopeful future. All of this is gift and grace. *But not for a moment should we be glib about the grace in grief.* For so many, it is a costly grace (Bonhoeffer 1959), emerging from agony and sorrow. I am very aware that describing the wholeness that may emerge from the brokenness of grief may sound like wishful thinking or happy talk. It may seem to mask or minimize the raw pain of grief. None of this is what I intend. Wholeness doesn't mean our losses cease to hurt. Wholeness doesn't mean that suffering can't touch us. It does. It will. But in everything, God works for good, bringing wholeness out of the brokenness, in love.

But how can God's love and grace be so present when we are suffering so painfully? This is both paradox and mystery. We will never understand fully. The best we can do is to somehow hold in tension both the suffering and the grace of grief. Retired Yale University professor Nicholas Wolterstorff struggled to hold this tension after the death of his son Eric in a mountain-climbing accident:

Suffering may do us good—may be a blessing, something to be thankful for. This I have learned. . . . In the valley of suffering, despair and bitterness are brewed. But there also character is made. The valley of suffering is the vale of soul-making. But now things slip and slide around. How do I tell my blessings? For what do I give thanks and for what do I lament? Am I sometimes to sorrow over my delight and sometimes to delight over my sorrow? And how do I sustain my "No" to my son's early death while accepting with gratitude the opportunity offered of becoming what otherwise I could never be? How do I receive my suffering as blessing while repulsing the obscene thought that God jiggled the mountain to make *me* better? (1987, 96–97)

Chaplain and writer Kate Braestrup poignantly expresses a similar struggle in her autobiography. Kate's husband, Drew, had had the dream of going to seminary and becoming a minister. Tragically, he was killed in an accident, leaving Kate and their four young children. In the course of her grieving, Kate made the decision to attend seminary herself, after which she was ordained a Unitarian Universalist minister and became the chaplain to the Maine Warden Service. She reflects on her journey since Drew's death:

Death alters the reality of our lives; the death of an intimate changes it completely. No part of my life, from my most ethereal notions of God to the most mundane detail of tooth brushing, was the same after Drew died. Life consisted of one rending novelty after another, as anyone who has lost a spouse can attest. Still, as time went on, some of those novelties proved to be blessings. And, like anyone who has survived the death of an intimate, I had to learn to live with a paradox. If Drew had lived, I would not have gone to seminary, would not be ordained, would not have become the warden service chaplain. There are places that would have gone unvisited and friends I would never have met, friends I now can't imagine doing without. So while on one hand there is my darling Drew, whom I will never cease to love and never cease to long for, on the other hand, there is a wonderful life that I enjoy and am grateful for. I can't make those two realities—what I've lost and what I've found—fit together in some tidy pattern of divine causality. I just have to hold them on the one hand and on the other, just like that. (2007, 202)

Grief is a complex experience, and some of it is mystery and paradox. We cannot understand it all, and so we must simply try to trust in "the love of Christ that surpasses knowledge, so that [we] may be filled with all the fullness of God" (Eph. 3:19).

In surprising, paradoxical, and sometimes painful ways, a wholeness may emerge from the brokenness of grief, through God's creative love. But the journey of grief is not marked only by God's creative activity. Because we are in relationship with God, we, too, are called to act in our grief, to help to bring wholeness from the brokenness. We may always carry the scars of our grief, as the risen Christ bore the marks of his suffering. But assured of the love of God in Christ, making all things new, we move into the future, where God beckons. In so doing we cocreate meaning and hope with God. This is an essential part of the work of grief. And it is blessed work. Jesus said, "Blessed are those who mourn, for they will be comforted" (Matt. 5:4). Truly we are blessed and comforted in our grief by the constant and abundant love of God.

Ministerial Perspective

In the first letter of Peter, we hear these challenging words: "Always be ready to make your defense to anyone who demands from you an accounting for the hope that is in you" (1 Peter 3:15). As ministers, we must accept this charge, and it is never more urgent than when people are grieving. Loss and subsequent grief can leave any of us, like Barry, struggling to find hope. We may not know how to keep living into a future so overshadowed by loss. We also may not know how to believe in God's abundant love in the midst of our pain. People often turn to their ministers to help them find hope after loss. This is a tremendously important task and responsibility. Indeed, pastoral theologian Donald Capps maintains that offering hope is the very definition of ministry: "Where other professionals may offer hope as a byproduct of what they do, the offer of hope is central to what pastors do. Oftentimes, it is all that they can offer. To be a pastor is to be a provider or agent of hope" (1995, 1).

I would like to propose three ways in which a minister may be an agent of hope for Barry. First, we cannot talk credibly to Barry about hope unless we have first acknowledged his painful reality. Hope begins with reality (Lester 1995). This is a very important point. Sometimes in our deep desire to relieve another's suffering, we may rush to reassurances that minimize or deny one's reality. For instance, we may say things like "Everything's going to be okay," or "This is a blessing in disguise." For many grieving people, such comments suggest that ministers either don't "get it" or cannot tolerate their deep pain; they offer little hope and can even lead to greater suffering. I remember attending a prayer service on the evening of September 11, 2001, the day of the horrific terrorist attacks on the United States. The minister preached on the passage "Do not let your hearts be troubled" (John 14:1). I am certain that this was a most earnest effort—under terrible circumstances—to comfort all of us. And yet I did not feel comfort. My heart was indeed deeply troubled, and I needed to hear words that acknowledged the stunning reality before I could move toward hope. Barry, too, needs people to acknowledge the extent and depth of his losses.

But, of course, we do not simply acknowledge the reality of suffering. Christian hope begins with the cross, but it does not end there. After we acknowledge the reality, we then help people to attend to where God is present and active, bringing wholeness out of brokenness, in love. This is the second way in which we might be agents of hope. Despite his great losses, Barry does not need to see life as bleak and to think small about his future. While he will likely always feel the great loss of Adam, Sam, and Ed, God is always present to him in abundantly loving ways, calling him "into an open-ended future" (Lester 1995, 2). This may be very difficult for Barry to imagine or to trust. For much of his life, he has experienced God as distant and perhaps even punishing. And so we do our best to remind Barry that he is loved abundantly by God. His relationships with Adam, Sam, and Ed were all manifestations of this abundant love. The other close relationships in his life reflect this abundant love. And in our efforts to offer understanding and compassion to Barry, God's abundant love is present.

God's abundant love for Barry is also present in his faith community. Therefore, the third way a minister can be an agent of hope for Barry is to help him draw on and strengthen his connection with this community. The Chinese writer Lusin has said, "Hope is like a road in the country; there was never a road, but when many people walk on it, the road comes into existence" (cited in Yutang 1942, 1087). As we seek hope in our grief, we need the witness and the companionship of others who have trodden the road before us. The Christian community has witnessed to hope in Christ and his resurrection promises for thousands of years. And this witness continues in each faith community today through individual and collective acts of being present, praying together, and offering care in Christ's name. Sometimes we may underestimate how the faith community incarnates God's love. But notice the many touching ways that Nicholas Wolterstorff's faith community was present to him, in Christian love, at the funeral for his son Eric:

> After the opening words, a shroud was placed over the coffin, simple but wonderfully beautiful, made a few years before by members of our congregation for the funeral of the friend with cancer. This was its first use. On the shroud over the coffin one of Eric's brothers placed lilies. The music was glorious, some of it sung by the congregation, some by the congregation in conjunction with a choir. . . . We celebrated the Eucharist, that sacrament of God's participation in our brokenness. We came forward successively in groups, standing in circles around the coffin, passing the signs of Christ's brokenness to each other. At the end, before we had committed Eric into the tender resurrected resurrecting hands of Jesus, I could not restrain myself from coming forward to express our deep appreciation for this outpouring of love and faith. . . . Now here I was, standing in front of that congregation, they too standing, tears streaming down my face and down theirs, tears answering to tears. (1987, 39–40)

Barry, too, is part of a wonderful faith community, and this community can be a tremendous source of hope for him. They all lost Ed; they can remember, honor, and pray for him together. They can walk together on the road to wholeness and meaning. And they can witness to each other that ultimate hope and ultimate meaning issue from the faithful love of God. Thus, we try to be agents of hope for Barry by acknowledging his painful reality, helping him to feel God's abundant love calling him into a hopeful future, and helping him to draw close to his community of faith, through whom God's faithful love is made manifest.

While being agents of hope for others in their grief is perhaps a minister's primary role, it is often an arduous one. We may be with people in the greatest pain of their lives. They may ask us unanswerable questions about God and suffering. We may feel the pressure to be "eternally hopeful" (Capps 1995, 3), even when we may be struggling with hope ourselves. What helps to sustain us in this challenging but critical ministry? Let me offer two thoughts. First, we must never let the hope of others reside ultimately with us. A friend of mine once worked in a challenging ministry setting and sometimes felt the pressure virtually to perform miracles for struggling people. What a relief it was for her when a colleague passionately reminded her, "You ain't Jesus! You ain't Jesus!" Likewise, we ain't Jesus. We do our best to offer hope and love while, like John the Baptist, we point always to the One who is greater than we are and the Lord of all hopefulness. And second, we must try to trust and hope that God is present to us, too, in abundantly loving ways. This is what sustains us in the hard work of grief care. In the midst of the great pain, paradox, and mystery of grief, we are loved, deeply and fully, by God.

Enfolded in God's Love

Throughout this book I have talked repeatedly of God's love. God's love is the ultimate secure base. God's love creates ultimate meaning from narrative disruption. God's love holds us in the brokenness of grief. God's abundant love brings hope and wholeness from this brokenness. But let's be honest. It is sometimes incredibly hard to know God's love, particularly if we have not known abundant love in our human relationships. It may also be hard to know God's love if we have been encouraged to think of God as primarily distant, judgmental, or punishing. Barry is struggling in this way. But it is never too late to know the love of God. How could it be, since nothing is impossible with God (Luke 1:37)? As we imagine ministering to Barry, on what further resources might we draw to help him know and trust more deeply in God's abundant love for him? In my own spiritual journey, I have always found it important and helpful to hear from others who have known God's love deeply. They help me to hope and trust more fully in God's timeless and abundant love. Julian of Norwich, a fourteenth-century English mystic, is such a person. Barry, too, may benefit from coming to hear some of the story and some of the words of Julian of Norwich.

We know little about the historical life of Julian of Norwich, including her actual name. She was twice visited by the Black Death and witnessed the effects of great political unrest, religious struggles, and poverty. At the age of thirty, over the course of a day's time, Julian experienced a series of sixteen visions, called *showings*. She wrote down her visions, as she felt God had instructed her to do, in what was the first book written in English by a woman. Julian's writings are a testament to the never-ending love of God and the hope such love instills.

According to Julian, we cannot fully know how deeply and totally loved we are by God, who "before he made us . . . loved us" (cited in Colledge & Walsh 1978, 283).[4] Being grounded in God's love is our natural state: "For our soul sits in God in true rest, and our soul stands in God in sure strength, and our soul is naturally rooted in God in endless love" (ibid., 289). God's love in Christ comforts us and protects us: "He is our clothing, who wraps and enfolds us for love, embraces us and shelters us, surrounds us for his love, which is so tender that he may never desert us" (ibid., 183).

Julian possessed a substantial understanding of humankind's sinful nature. Yet she understood God as never blaming people for sin and sin as never overcoming God's love for God's creation. Julian asked for more understanding about sin and its destructive effects, and Jesus replied to her, in the famous words that have brought comfort to so many, "Sin is necessary, but all will be well, and all will be well, and every kind of thing will be well" (ibid., 225). Because of God's love, we will not be ultimately overcome by any suffering or trial.

> He did not say: You will not be troubled, you will not be belaboured, you will not be disquieted; but he said: You will not be overcome. God wants us to pay attention to these words, and always to be strong in faithful trust, in well-being and in woe, for he loves us and delights in us, and so he wishes us to love him and delight in him and trust greatly in him, and all will be well. (ibid., 315)

Julian of Norwich has much to say to those who grieve.[5] She was in a long and faithful relationship with God (Flinders 1993); her writing emerged through her prayer and conversations with God over twenty years. In this time, her understanding of the meaning of her showings evolved and deepened. God was her constant partner in this ongoing process of meaning-making. And the ultimate meaning that Julian came to know was the endless, boundless love of God for all of God's creation: "Know it well, love was his meaning" (Colledge & Walsh 1978, 342). God is also in faithful relationship with Barry and with all of us. As we grieve and seek meaning after loss, God is our faithful and loving partner. And the meaning that we, too, must cling to is that God is love. Each of us is, in Julian's words, "endlessly loved with an endless love" (ibid., 308). We will suffer and grieve in this life, but in the deepest possible sense, all will be well, because God loves us. This is why we hope.

The Mosaic of Grief

In the previous chapter, I said that mosaics emerge from brokenness. This is true. Fragments, remnants, shards, and pieces are the medium of mosaic art. And yet, by definition, the mosaic itself is always more than the pieces. Its beauty lies precisely in the whole that emerges from the fragments, a whole that is greater, fuller, and richer than the sum of the parts.

The mosaic of grief emerges from the brokenness we endure as we suffer and grieve. When we reflect on our mosaic of grief, perhaps we wish that we could pluck out certain fragments or shards. If we could, we might undo terribly painful losses and escape the suffering we have known. But we can't. Each experience is forever part of our story, and each fragment is forever part of our mosaic of grief. But, in time, our mosaic of grief begins to yield something that is greater than the pieces. Gradually, a wholeness emerges that is built from all of the pieces and bigger than any of them.

As we reflect on the wholeness that emerges from the brokenness of grief, I would like to say a word about the cover of this book. The picture is entitled *Nebula*. A nebula is a cloud of gases and dust particles. Nebulae form from all the debris that blankets the universe; for instance, many nebulae emerge from the explosion of stars. As we have learned from space photographs, nebulae are often stunningly beautiful. But they are not static. Slowly, over billions of years, a nebula gets smaller, causing its inner temperature to rise. When the temperature reaches a critical point, the nebula implodes. But this is not the end of the story. Something new issues from the implosion. Indeed, *countless new stars that form in our universe emerge from nebulae.* Loss is part of all of life, even at the levels of dust particles and stars. The astonishing universe we see today was born of loss and destruction unfolding over eons. But a wholeness continues to emerge, slowly, from all the loss. The gaseous remnants, the dusty fragments sometimes become new stars.

In his poem "Incantata," the poet Paul Muldoon proposes that art "builds from pain, from misery, from a deep-seated hurt, / a monument to the human heart / that shines like a golden dome among roofs rain-glazed / and leaden" (1994, 19). Notice he does not suggest that art takes away pain, misery, and hurt. Rather, it builds from them a golden monument to the heart. So it is with the mosaic of grief. It is a monument to our strength, to our resilience, to our efforts to hang on in our suffering and to hope for the wholeness that will eventually emerge. But we do not build this monument alone; it is cocreated, through our love for one another and through God's love for all. Vincent Van Gogh once said, "There is nothing more truly artistic than to love people." In our love and compassion for those who grieve, we are artists, cocreating the mosaic of grief. Our work is not to remove or smooth out all the broken pieces, but rather to help the pieces come together in a wholeness that brings hope because it is grounded in the love of God.

But, of course, in this art we are always apprentices, learning at the feet of the Master of love. As I was finishing this book, I happened upon a small craft shop in western North Carolina. One of the local crafts on display was a standing mosaic cross, made of ceramic fragments and shards. What a perfect image with which to conclude this book. Jesus Christ, broken for us, knows our suffering and pain intimately. As we care for ourselves and others in grief, we can do no better than to stand at the foot of the cross, feeling the compassion of Christ and trusting in God's abundant love, which raised Christ from the dead and which is our hope in suffering. In poignant words that beautifully echo Julian of Norwich, this abundant love of God is described by Abbé Henri de Tourville, a spiritual director in France in the nineteenth century:

Accustom yourself to the wonderful thought that God loves you with a tenderness, a generosity, and an intimacy which surpasses all your dreams. Give yourself up with joy to a loving confidence in God and have courage to believe firmly that God's action towards you is a masterpiece of partiality and love. Rest tranquilly in this abiding conviction. (1939, 58)

God, the Master Artist, is constantly at work in all our lives, bringing hope out of brokenness, in love. All will be well.

❖   ❖   ❖

Questions for Reflection

1. Think about your own experiences of loss and grief in relational perspective. What are the relationships in your life that you have grieved? What have been the effects of these losses on your sense of self and of your future? When you have grieved, have you felt supported and cared for by others? How has your grief changed you in ways that have perhaps changed your relationships?

2. In your times of grief, how have you experienced God? Have you felt the abundant love of God holding you and surrounding you, bringing wholeness out of brokenness and calling you into a hopeful future? Has God been "an abiding Presence that sustains . . . even in the midst of things that are passing away" (Bennett 1997, 31)?

3. Like Barry, have you ever struggled after loss to feel hope for your future? Have you ever wondered if life is perhaps more to be endured than to be enjoyed? Have you sometimes experienced God as a distant or unfeeling figure? If so, how might the words of Julian of Norwich help you to trust more deeply that you are "endlessly loved with an endless love"?

4. In your times of grief, who has communicated God's abundant love to you? Who has helped you to create meaning that is grounded in God's love for you?

5. If Barry sought your help and support, how might you respond to him, both initially and over time, in ways that might help him to sense God's abundant love for him?

6. How might Barry's faith community respond to him in ways that could help him to feel and to trust God's love in the midst of his grief, calling him into a hopeful future?

7. What questions or ideas flowing from this chapter might you want to bring to your prayer or to conversations with trusted friends or colleagues?

Bibliography

Adams, C., & M. Fortune, eds. 1996. *Violence against Women and Children: A Christian Theological Sourcebook.* New York: Continuum.

Ainsworth, M. D. 1967. *Infancy in Uganda: Infant Care and the Growth of Attachment.* Baltimore: Johns Hopkins University Press.

———. 1985. "Attachments across the Life Span." *Bulletin of the New York Academy of Medicine* 61:792–812.

Ainsworth, M. D., M. Blehar, E. Waters, & S. Wall. 1978. *Patterns of Attachment: A Psychological Study of the Strange Situation.* Hillsdale, N.J.: Erlbaum.

Ano, G. G., & E. B. Vasconcelles. 2005. "Religious Coping and Psychological Adjustment to Stress: A Meta-Analysis." *Journal of Clinical Psychology* 61:461–80.

Archer, J. 2008. "Theories of Grief: Past, Present, and Future Perspectives." In Stroebe, Hansson, Schut, & Stroebe 2008, 45–65.

Attig, T. 1996. *How We Grieve: Relearning the World.* New York: Oxford University Press.

———. 2001. "Relearning the World: Making and Finding Meanings." In Neimeyer 2001a, 33–53.

Augsburger, D. W. 1986. *Pastoral Counseling across Cultures.* Philadelphia: Westminster.

Bair, D. 2003. *Jung: A Biography.* New York: Back Bay Books.

Barthes, R. 1966. "Introduction to the Structural Analysis of the Narrative." Occasional paper, Centre for Contemporary Cultural Studies, University of Birmingham. Stenciled. S/Z, 1970. Translated by Richard Miller. New York: Hill & Wang, 1974.

Bartholomew, K., & P. Shaver. 1998. "Methods of Assessing Adult Attachment: Do They Converge?" In J. A. Simpson & W. S. Rholes, eds., *Attachment Theory and Close Relationships*, 25–45. New York: Guilford.

Basgelen, N., & Ergec, R. 2000. *Belkis/Zeugma, Halfeti, Rumkale: A Last Look at History*. Istanbul: Archaeology and Art Publications.

Bennett, P. 1997. *Let Yourself Be Loved*. Mahwah, N.J.: Paulist.

Bhui, K., M. King, S. Dein, & W. O'Connor. 2008. "Ethnicity and Religious Coping with Mental Distress." *Journal of Mental Health* 17:141–51.

Boerner, K., C. Wortman, & G. Bonanno. 2005. "Resilient or At Risk? A Four-Year Study of Older Adults Who Initially Showed High or Low Distress Following Conjugal Loss." *Journals of Gerontology Series B: Psychological Sciences and Social Sciences* 60:67–73.

Bonanno, G. A., C. B. Wortman, D. R. Lehman, R. G. Tweed, M. Haring, J. Sonnega, D. Carr, & R. M. Nesse. 2002. "Resilience to Loss and Chronic Grief: A Prospective Study from Preloss to Eighteen-Months Postloss." *Journal of Personality and Social Psychology* 83:1150–164.

Bonanno, G. A., C. B. Wortman, & R. M. Nesse. 2004. "Prospective Patterns of Resilience and Maladjustment during Widowhood." *Psychology and Aging* 19:260–71.

Bonhoeffer, D. 1959. *The Cost of Discipleship*. New York: Macmillan.

Boss, P. 1999a. *Ambiguous Loss: Learning to Live with Unresolved Grief*. Cambridge: Harvard University Press.

———. 1999b. "Ambiguous Loss: Living with Frozen Grief." *Harvard Mental Health Letter*, Nov. 16:4–6.

Bowlby, J. 1969. *Attachment and Loss*. Vol. 1, *Attachment*. New York: Basic Books.

———. 1973. *Attachment and Loss*. Vol. 2, *Separation*. New York: Basic Books.

———. 1979. *The Making and Breaking of Affectional Bonds*. London: Tavistock.

———. 1980. *Attachment and Loss*. Vol. 3, *Loss*. New York: Basic Books.

———. 1988. *A Secure Base: Parent-Child Attachment and Healthy Human Development*. New York: Basic Books.

Bowlby, J., & C. Parkes. 1970. "Separation and Loss within the Family." In E. J. Anthony, ed., *The Child in His Family*, 197–216. New York: Wiley.

Braestrup, K. 2007. *Here If You Need Me*. New York: Little, Brown.

Bretherton, I., & K. A. Munholland. 1999. "Internal Working Models in Attachment Relationships: A Construct Revisited." In Cassidy & Shaver 1999, 89–111.

Buechner, F. 1999. *The Eyes of the Heart: A Memoir of the Lost and Found*. New York: HarperCollins.

———. 2008. *The Yellow Leaves: A Miscellany*. Louisville: Westminster John Knox.

Byron, L. 1973. *Don Juan*. Edited by T. G. Steffan, E. Steffan, & W. W. Pratt. New York: Penguin.

Calhoun, L., & R. Tedeschi. 2001. "Posttraumatic Growth: The Positive Lessons of Loss." In Neimeyer 2001a, 157–72.

Cannon, K., B. Harrison, C. Heyward, A. Isasi-Díaz, B. Johnson, M. Pellauer, & N. Richardson. 1985. *God's Fierce Whimsy*. New York: Pilgrim.

Caplan, G. 1964. *Principles of Preventive Psychiatry*. New York: Basic Books.

Capps, D. 1995. *Agents of Hope: A Pastoral Psychology*. Minneapolis: Fortress Press.

Carmichael, M. 2009. "Who Says Stress Is Bad for You?" *Newsweek*, February 23, 47–50.

Cash, R. 2006. "World without Sound." On *Black Cadillac* (audio CD). Capitol Records 48738.

Cassidy, J., & P. Shaver, eds. 1999. *Handbook of Attachment: Theory, Research, and Clinical Applications*. New York: Guilford.

Cinnirella, M., & K. M. Loewenthal. 1999. "Religious and Ethnic Group Influences on Beliefs about Mental Illness: A Qualitative Interview Study." *British Journal of Medicine and Psychology* 72:505–24.

Cohen, L. 1992. "Anthem." On *The Future* (audio CD). Columbia-Sony CK 53226.

Cole, B. S. 2005. "Spiritually-Focused Psychotherapy for People Diagnosed with Cancer: A Pilot Study." *Mental Health, Religion and Culture* 8:217–26.

Conger, R. D., & M. B. Donnellan. 2007. "An Interactionist Perspective on the Socioeconomic Context of Human Development." *Annual Review of Psychology* 58:175–99.

Cook, A. S., & K. A. Oltjenbruns, 1998. "The Bereaved Family." In A. S. Cook & K. A. Oltjenbruns, eds., *Dying and Grieving: Life Span and Family Perspectives*, 91–115. Fort Worth: Harcourt Brace.

Cook, J. A., & D. W. Wimberly. 1983. "If I Should Die before I Wake: Religious Commitment and Adjustment to the Death of a Child." *Journal for the Scientific Study of Religion* 22:222–38.

Crits-Christoph, P., L. Siqueland, J. Blaine, A. Frank, L. Luborsky, L. Onken, L. Muenz, M. Thase, et al. 1999. "Psychosocial Treatments for Cocaine Dependence." *Archives of General Psychiatry* 56:493–502.

Darwin, C. 1872. *The Expression of the Emotions in Man and Animals*. London: Murray.

Dean, J. 1988. "Grief and Attachment." *Journal of Religion and Health* 27, no. 2:157–65.

De Buzareingues, A. F., B. Jones, & E. Arledge, producers. 2000. *Lost Roman Treasure*. DVD. Gedeon Programmes.

DeLongis, A., J. Coyne, G. Dakof, S. Folkman, & R. Lazarus. 1982. "Relationship of Daily Hassles, Uplifts, and Major Life Events to Health Status." *Health Psychology* 1:119–36.

DeSpelder, L. A., & A. L. Strickland. 2005. *The Last Dance: Encountering Death and Dying*. 7th ed. New York: McGraw-Hill.

De Tourville, A. H. 1939. *Letters of Direction: Thoughts on the Spiritual Life from the Letters of the Abbé de Tourville*. London: Continuum.

Deutsch, A. 1975. "Observations of a Sidewalk Ashram." *Archives of General Psychiatry* 32:166–75.

Dickinson, E. 1924. *The Complete Poems of Emily Dickinson*. Boston: Little, Brown.

Doka, K. 2008. "Disenfranchised Grief in Historical and Cultural Perspective." In Stroebe, Hansson, Schut, & Stroebe 2008, 223–40.

———, ed. 1989. *Disenfranchised Grief: Recognizing Hidden Sorrow*. Lexington, Mass.: Lexington.

———, ed. 2002. *Disenfranchised Grief: New Directions, Challenges, and Strategies for Practice*. Champaign, Ill.: Research Press.

Doll, D., & D. Bowley. 2008. "Veterans' Health—Surviving Acute Injuries Is Not Enough." *The Lancet* 371:1053–55.

Edwards, E. 2006. *Saving Graces: Finding Solace and Strength from Friends and Strangers*. New York: Broadway.

Eliot, T. S. 1971. *The Complete Poems and Plays: 1909–1950*. New York: Harcourt, Brace & World.

Emerson, E. W., & W. E. Forbes, eds. 1911. *Journals of Ralph Waldo Emerson with Annotations, 1841–1844*. Boston: Houghton Mifflin.

English, B. 2009. "Bereaved Fathers Find Healing in Friendship." *Boston Globe*, April 29, A1, A6.

Erikson, E., J. Erikson, & H. Kivnick. 1986. *Vital Involvement in Old Age*. New York: Norton.

"Fast Facts: The Faces of Poverty." 2006. UN Millennium Project. http://www.unmillenniumproject.org/resources/fastfacts_e.htm, accessed October 19, 2009.

Feeney, J. 1999. "Adult Romantic Attachment and Couple Relationships." In Cassidy & Shaver 1999, 355–77.

Field, N. 2006. "Unresolved Grief and Continuing Bonds: An Attachment Perspective." *Death Studies* 30, no. 8:739–56.

Field, N., B. Gao, & L. Paderna. 2005. "Continuing Bonds in Bereavement: An Attachment Theory Based Perspective." *Death Studies* 29:277–99.

Flinders, C. L. 1993. *Enduring Grace: Living Portraits of Seven Women Mystics.* New York: HarperCollins.

Folkman, S. 1984. "Personal Control and Stress and Coping Processes: A Theoretical Analysis." *Journal of Personality and Social Psychology* 46:839–52.

Fortune, M. 1987. *Keeping the Faith: Guidance for Christian Women Facing Abuse.* New York: HarperCollins.

Fraley, R. C., & P. R. Shaver. 1999. "Loss and Bereavement: Attachment Theory and Recent Controversies concerning 'Grief Work' and the Nature of Detachment." In Cassidy & Shaver 1999, 735–59.

Frankl, V. 1984 [1959]. *Man's Search for Meaning.* New York: Simon & Schuster.

Frantz, T., M. Farrell, & B. Trolley. 2001. "Positive Outcomes of Losing a Loved One." In Neimeyer 2001a, 191–209.

Freud, S. 1957 [1917]. "Mourning and Melancholia." In J. Strachey, ed. and trans., *The Standard Edition of the Complete Psychological Works of Sigmund Freud,* 14:243–58. London: Hogarth.

Gaines, R. 1997. "Detachment and Continuity: The Two Tasks of Mourning." *Contemporary Psychoanalysis* 33:549–571.

Galanter, M. 1979. "The 'Moonies': A Psychological Study of Conversion and Membership in a Contemporary Religious Sect." *American Journal of Psychiatry* 136:165–70.

Ganzevoort, R. R. 1998. "Religious Coping Reconsidered, Part 1: An Integrated Approach. *Journal of Psychology and Theology* 26:260–75.

Gass, K. A. 1987. "The Health of Conjugally Bereaved Older Widows: The Role of Appraisal, Coping and Resources." *Research in Nursing and Health* 10:39–47.

Goodstein, L. 2001. "A Nation Challenged: Religion; As Attacks' Impact Recedes, a Return to Religion as Usual." *New York Times,* November 26, A1.

Goss, R. E., & D. Klass. 2005. *Dead but Not Lost: Grief Narratives in Religious Traditions*. Walnut Creek, Calif.: AltaMira.

Granqvist, P., & L. Kirkpatrick. 2004. "Religious Conversion and Perceived Childhood Attachment: A Meta-Analysis." *International Journal for the Psychology of Religion* 14, no. 4:223–50.

Grene, D., & R. Lattimore, eds. 1956. *The Complete Greek Tragedies*. Vol. 3, *Euripides*. Chicago: University of Chicago Press.

Hagman, G. 1993. *The Psychoanalytic Understanding and Treatment of Double Parent Loss*. Paper presented at the fall meeting of the American Psychoanalytic Association, New York.

Hagman, G. 1995a. "Death of a Selfobject: Towards a Self Psychology of the Mourning Process." In A. Goldberg, ed., *Progress in Self Psychology*, vol. 11, 189–205. Hillsdale, N.J.: Analytic Press.

Hagman, G. 1995b. "Mourning: A Review and Reconsideration." *International Journal of Psychoanalysis* 76:909–25.

Hagman, G. 1996a. "Bereavement and Neurosis." *Journal of American Academy of Psychoanalysis* 23:635–53.

Hagman, G. 1996b. "Flight from the Subjectivity of the Other: Pathological Adaptation to Early Parent Loss." In A. Goldberg, ed., *Progress in Self Psychology*, vol. 12, 207–19). Hillsdale, N.J.: Analytic Press.

Hagman, G. 2001. "Beyond Decathexis: Toward a New Psychoanalytic Understanding and Treatment of Mourning." In Neimeyer 2001a, 13–31.

Haun, D. 1977. "Perception of the Bereaved, Clergy, and Funeral Directors concerning Bereavement." *Dissertation Abstracts International* A37:6791A.

Havel, V. 1990. *Disturbing the Peace*. Translated by Paul Wilson. New York: Alfred A. Knopf.

Hoge, C. W., D. McGurk, J. L. Thomas, A. L. Cox, C. C. Engel, & C. A. Castro. 2008. "Mild Traumatic Brain Injury in U.S. Soldiers Returning from Iraq." *New England Journal of Medicine* 358:453–63.

Howe, L. 1995. *The Image of God: A Theology for Pastoral Care and Counseling*. Nashville: Abingdon.

———. 2000. *A Pastor in Every Pew: Equipping Laity for Pastoral Care*. Valley Forge, Pa.: Judson.

Hummel, L. 2003. "'Practical Bearings': A Pastoral Theology of Religious Coping Research." *Journal of Pastoral Theology* 13:46–62.

Jason, M., J. Meier, & M. Jacobs, executive producers. 2009. *Freedom Songs: The Music of the Civil Rights Movement*. DVD. Rhythm Mass Productions.

Jenkins, R. A., & K. I. Pargament. 1988. "Cognitive Appraisals in Cancer Patients." *Social Science and Medicine* 26:625–33.

Jones, K. B. 2001. *Rest in the Storm: Self-Care Strategies for Clergy and Other Caregivers.* Valley Forge, Pa.: Judson.

Jordan, J., A. Kaplan, J. Miller, I. Stiver, & J. Surrey. 1991. *Women's Growth in Connection: Writings from the Stone Center.* New York: Guilford.

Josselson, R. 2007. "Introduction." In R. Josselson, A. Lieblich, & D. McAdams, eds., *The Meaning of Others: Narrative Studies of Relationships*, 3–10. Washington, D.C.: American Psychological Association.

Jubis, R. 1991. *An Attachment-Theoretical Approach to Understanding Children's Conceptions of God.* Unpublished doctoral dissertation, University of Denver, Denver, Colorado.

Julian of Norwich. 1978. *Showings.* Translated by E. Colledge & J. Walsh. Mahwah, N.J.: Paulist.

Kaplan, H., B. Sadock, & J. Grebb. 1994. *Kaplan and Sadock's Synopsis of Psychiatry.* 7th ed. Baltimore: Williams & Wilkins.

Kaplan, L. 1995. *No Voice Is Ever Wholly Lost.* New York: Simon & Schuster.

Kaufman, G. 1981. *The Theological Imagination.* Philadelphia: Westminster.

Kelley, M. 2003. "Bereavement and Grief Related to a Significant Death: A Psychological and Theological Study of Attachment Styles and Religious Coping." *Dissertation Abstracts International* 63, no. 10:3607A.

———. 2009. "Loss through the Lens of Attachment to God." *Journal of Spirituality in Mental Health* 11:88–106.

Kennedy, K. 2008. *Being Catholic Now: Prominent Americans Talk about Change in the Church and the Quest for Meaning.* New York: Crown.

Kim, H., D. Sherman, & S. Taylor. 2008. "Culture and Social Support." *American Psychologist* 63:518–26.

Kirkpatrick, L. 1992. "An Attachment-Theoretical Approach to the Psychology of Religion." *International Journal for the Psychology of Religion* 2, no. 1:3–28.

———. 1999. "Attachment and Religious Representations and Behavior." In Cassidy & Shaver 1999, 803–22.

———. 2005. *Attachment, Evolution, and the Psychology of Religion.* New York: Guilford.

Kirkpatrick, L., & P. Shaver. 1990. "Attachment Theory and Religion: Childhood Attachments, Religious Beliefs, and Conversion." *Journal for the Scientific Study of Religion* 29:315–34.

———. 1992. "An Attachment-Theoretical Approach to Romantic Love and Religious Belief." *Personality and Social Psychology Bulletin* 18, no. 3:266–75.

Klass, D., & R. Goss. 1999. "Spiritual Bonds to the Dead in Cross-Cultural and Historical Perspective: Comparative Religion and Modern Grief." *Death Studies* 23:547–67.

Klass, D., P. Silverman, & S. Nickman, eds. 1996. *Continuing Bonds: New Understandings of Grief.* Philadelphia: Taylor & Francis.

Komaroff, A. 2009. "The Usual Suspect." *Newsweek*, February 23, 52, 55.

Kübler-Ross, E. 1969. *On Death and Dying*. New York: Scribner.

Kuhn, D. 2002. "A Pastoral Counselor Looks at Silence as a Factor in Disenfranchised Grief." In Doka 2002, 119–26.

Lambert, W., L. Triandis, & M. Wolf. 1959. "Some Correlates of Beliefs in the Malevolence and Benevolence of Supernatural Beings: A Cross-Societal Study." *Journal of Abnormal and Social Psychology* 58:162–69.

Lamott, A. 2005. *Plan B: Further Thoughts on Faith*. New York: Riverhead.

Lester, A. 1995. *Hope in Pastoral Care and Counseling*. Louisville: Westminster John Knox.

Lewis, C. S. 1961. *A Grief Observed*. New York: Bantam.

Lindemann, E. 1944. "Symptomatology and Management of Acute Grief." *American Journal of Psychiatry* 101:141–48.

Little, D., & S. B. Twiss. 1973. "Basic Terms in the Study of Religious Ethics." In G. Outka & J. P. Reeder Jr., eds., *Religion and Morality: A Collection of Essays*, 35–77. New York: Anchor.

Loewenthal, K. M., & M. Cinnirella. 1999. "Beliefs about the Efficacy of Religious, Medical and Psychotherapeutic Interventions for Depression and Schizophrenia among Women from Different Cultural-Religious Groups in Great Britain." *Transcultural Psychiatry* 36:491–504.

Loewenthal, K. M., M. Cinnirella, G. Evdoka, & P. Murphy. 2001. "Faith Conquers All? Beliefs about the Role of Religious Factors in Coping with Depression among Different Cultural-Religious Groups in the UK." *British Journal of Medicine and Psychology* 74:293–303.

Lopez, B., & T. Pohrt. 1990. *Crow and Weasel*. San Francisco: North Point.

Loveland, G. 1968. "The Effects of Bereavement on Certain Religious Attitudes." *Sociological Symposium* 1:17–27.

Main, M., & R. Goldwyn. 1984. *Adult Attachment Scoring and Classification Systems*. Unpublished manuscript, University of California at Berkeley.

———. 1998. *Adult Attachment Scoring and Classification Systems*. 2nd ed. Unpublished manuscript, University of California at Berkeley.

Main, M., & J. Solomon. 1986. "Discovery of a New, Insecure Disorganized/Disoriented Attachment Pattern." In T. B. Brazelton & M. Yogman, eds., *Affective Development in Infancy*, 95–124. Norwood, N.J.: Ablex.

———. 1990. "Procedures for Identifying Infants as Disorganized/Disoriented during the Ainsworth Strange Situation." In M. T. Greenberg,

D. Cicchetti, & E. M. Cummings, eds., *Attachment in the Preschool Years*, 121–60. Chicago: University of Chicago Press.

Martin, S. 2008. "Money Is the Top Stressor for Americans." *Monitor on Psychology* 39:28–29.

Martin, T., & K. Doka. 2000. *Men Don't Cry . . . Women Do: Transcending Gender Stereotypes of Grief.* Philadelphia: Brunner/Mazel.

Marty, M. E. 1983. *A Cry of Absence: Reflections for the Winter of the Heart.* San Francisco: Harper & Row.

Mattis, J. S., D. L. Fontenot, & C. A. Hatcher-Kay. 2003. "Religiosity, Racism, and Dispositional Optimism among African Americans." *Personality and Individual Differences* 34:1025–38.

Maynard, J. 2006. *Transfiguring Loss: Julian of Norwich as a Guide for Survivors of Traumatic Grief.* Cleveland: Pilgrim.

McAdams, D. P. 1993. *The Stories We Live By: Personal Myths and the Making of the Self.* New York: William Morrow.

McCann, L., & L. A. Pearlman. 1990. "Vicarious Traumatization: A Framework for Understanding the Psychological Effects of Working with Victims." *Journal of Traumatic Stress* 3:131–49.

McConnell, K., K. Pargament, C. Ellison, & K. Flannelly. 2006. "Examining the Links between Spiritual Struggles and Symptoms of Psychopathology in a National Sample." *Journal of Clinical Psychology* 62:1469–84.

Middlebrooks, J. S., & N. C. Audage. 2008. *The Effects of Childhood Stress on Health across the Lifespan.* Atlanta: Centers for Disease Control and Prevention, National Center for Injury Prevention and Control.

Middleton, W., A. Moylan, B. Raphael, P. Burnett, & N. Martinek. 1993. "An International Perspective on Bereavement Related Concepts." *Australian and New Zealand Journal of Psychiatry* 27, no. 3:457–63.

Miller, M. C., ed. 2007a. "The Spiritual Side of Recovery." *Harvard Mental Health Letter* 24, no. 4 (October): 6.

———, ed. 2007b. "Research Suggests Why Stress May Add Pounds." *Harvard Mental Health Letter* 24, no. 6 (December): 7.

———, ed. 2008a. "Getting Help for Post-combat Mental Health Problems." *Harvard Mental Health Letter* 24, no. 10 (April): 6.

———, ed. 2008b. "Behavioral Cognitive Therapy for Addictions." *Harvard Mental Health Letter* 24, no. 11 (May): 5.

———, ed. 2008c. "The 'Forgotten Bereaved.'" *Harvard Mental Health Letter* 25, no. 3 (September): 6.

Miner, M. 2007. "Back to the Basics in Attachment to God: Revisiting Theory in Light of Theology." *Journal of Psychology and Theology* 35, no. 2:112–22.

Mishler, E. 1986. *Research Interviewing: Context and Narrative.* Cambridge: Harvard University Press.

Mitchell, K., & H. Anderson. 1983. *All Our Losses, All Our Griefs.* Philadelphia: Westminster.

Moltmann, J. 2004. *In the End—the Beginning: The Life of Hope.* Translated by Margaret Kohl. Minneapolis: Fortress Press.

Muldoon, P. 1994. *The Annals of Chile: Poems.* New York: Farrar, Straus & Giroux.

Neimeyer, R. 1999. "Narrative Strategies in Grief Therapy." *Journal of Constructivist Psychology* 12:65–85.

———. 2000. "Narrative Disruptions in the Construction of the Self." In R. Neimeyer & J. Raskin, eds., *Constructions of Disorder: Meaning-Making Frameworks for Psychotherapy*, 207–42. Washington, D.C.: American Psychological Association.

———, ed. 2001a. *Meaning Reconstruction and the Experience of Loss.* Washington, D.C.: American Psychological Association.

———. 2001b. "Preface." In Neimeyer 2001a, xi–xiii.

———. 2001c. "Introduction: Meaning Reconstruction and Loss." In Neimeyer 2001a, 1–9.

———. 2001d. "The Language of Loss: Grief Therapy as a Process of Meaning Reconstruction." In Neimeyer 2001a, 261–92.

———. 2005. "Growing through Grief: Constructing Coherence in Narratives of Loss." In D. Winter & L. Viney, eds., *Personal Construct Psychotherapy: Advances in Theory, Practice and Research*, 111–26. London: Whurr.

Neimeyer, R., & N. Keesee. 1998. "Dimensions of Diversity in the Reconstruction of Meaning." In K. Doka & J. Davidson, eds., *Living with Grief: Who We Are, How We Grieve*, 223–37. Philadelphia: Brunner/Mazel.

Neimeyer, R., H. Prigerson, & B. Davies. 2002. "Mourning and Meaning." *American Behavioral Scientist* 46, no. 2:235–51.

Ovid. *Tristia.* 1975. Translated by L. R. Lind. Athens: University of Georgia Press.

Pargament, K. 1997. *The Psychology of Religion and Coping: Theory, Research, Practice.* New York: Guilford.

Pargament, K. I. 2007. *Spiritually Integrated Psychotherapy: Understanding and Addressing the Sacred.* New York: Guilford.

Pargament, K., & H. Abu Raiya. 2007. "A Decade of Research on the Psychology of Religion and Coping: Things We Assumed and Lessons We Learned." *Psyke & Logos* 28:742–66.

Pargament, K., D. S. Ensing, K. Falgout, H. Olsen, B. Reilly, K. Van Haitsma, & R. Warren. 1990. "God Help Me: (I): Religious Coping Efforts as Predictors of the Outcomes to Significant Negative Life Events." *American Journal of Community Psychology* 18:793–824.

Pargament, K., H. G. Koenig, & L. M. Perez. 2000. "The Many Methods of Religious Coping: Development and Initial Validation of the RCOPE." *Journal of Clinical Psychology* 56:519–43.

Pargament, K., H. G. Koenig, N. Tarakeshwar, & J. Hahn. 2001. "Religious Struggle as a Predictor of Mortality among Medically Ill Elderly Patients: A Two-Year Longitudinal Study." *Archives of Internal Medicine* 161:1881–85.

————. 2004. "Religious Coping Methods as Predictors of Psychological, Physical, and Spiritual Outcomes among Medically Ill Elderly Patients: A Two-Year Longitudinal Study." *Journal of Health Psychology* 9:713–30.

Pargament, K., N. Murray-Swank, G. Magyar, & G. Ano. 2005. "Spiritual Struggle: A Phenomenon of Interest to Psychology and Religion." In W. R. Miller & H. D. Delaney, eds., *Judeo-Christian Perspectives on Psychology: Human Nature, Motivation, and Change*, 245-68. Washington, D.C.: American Psychological Association.

Pargament, K., & S. M. Saunders. 2007. "Introduction to the Special Issue on Spirituality and Psychotherapy." *Journal of Clinical Psychology* 63:903–7.

Pargament, K., B. Smith, H. Koenig, & L. Perez. 1998. "Patterns of Positive and Negative Religious Coping with Major Life Stressors." *Journal for the Scientific Study of Religion* 37:710–24.

Park, C., & L. Cohen. 1993. "Religious and Nonreligious Coping with the Death of a Friend." *Cognitive Therapy and Research* 17:561–77.

Park, C., L. Cohen, & R. Murch. 1996. "Assessment and Prediction of Stress-Related Growth." *Journal of Personality* 64, no. 1:71–105.

Parkes, C. M. 1993. "Bereavement as a Psychosocial Transition: Processes of Adaptation to Change." In M. Stroebe, W. Stroebe, & R. O. Hansson, eds., *Handbook of Bereavement: Theory, Research and Intervention*, 91–101. New York: Cambridge University Press.

————. 1996. *Bereavement: Studies of Grief in Adult Life*. 3rd ed. Philadelphia: Routledge.

————. 2001. "A Historical Overview of the Scientific Study of Bereavement." In Stroebe, Hansson, Stroebe, & Schut 2001a, 25–45.

Parry, A., & R. Doan. 1994. *Story Re-visions: Narrative Therapy in the Postmodern World*. New York: Guilford.

Persico, J. 2008. *Franklin and Lucy: President Roosevelt, Mrs. Rutherfurd, and the Other Remarkable Women in His Life*. New York: Random House.

Polkinghorne, D. 1988. *Narrative Knowing and the Human Sciences*. Albany: State University of New York Press.

Pollock, G. 1989. *The Mourning-Liberation Process*. Madison, Conn.: International Universities Press.

Potvin, R. 1977. "Adolescent God Images." *Review of Religious Research* 19:43–53.

"Poverty: At a Glance." 2009. World Bank. http://go.worldbank.org/2UJWJC2XG0, accessed October 19, 2009.

Price, R. H., J. N. Choi, & A. D. Vinokur. 2002. "Links in the Chain of Adversity Following Job Loss: How Financial Strain and Loss of Personal Control Lead to Depression, Impaired Functioning, and Poor Health." *Journal of Occupational Health Psychology* 7:302–12.

Richards, T. A. 2001. "Spiritual Resources Following a Partner's Death from AIDS." In Neimeyer 2001a, 173–90.

Rohner, R. 1975. *They Love Me, They Love Me Not*. New Haven, Conn.: Human Relations Area Files Press.

Roos, S. 2002. *Chronic Sorrow: A Living Loss*. New York: Brunner-Routledge.

Rosenblatt, P. 2001. "A Social Constructionist Perspective on Cultural Differences in Grief." In Stroebe, Hansson, Stroebe, & Schut 2001a, 285–300.

Schaefer, J., & R. Moos. 1992. "Life Crises and Personal Growth." In B. Carpenter, ed., *Personal Coping: Theory, Research, and Application*, 149–70. Westport, Conn.: Praeger.

Shaha, A., & D. Loeterman. 2009. "Can You Cheat Death?" *Newsweek*, June 22, 68.

Shakespeare, W. 1984. *King Richard II*. Edited by M. Clamp. 1984. Cambridge: Cambridge University Press.

———. 1968. *Macbeth*. Edited by J. D. Wilson. 1968. Cambridge: Cambridge University Press.

Shane, M., & E. Shane. 1990. "Object Loss and Selfobject Loss: A Contribution to Understanding Mourning and the Failure to Mourn." *Annual of Psychoanalysis* 18:115–31.

Shapiro, E. 1996. "Grief in Freud's Life: Reconceptualizing Bereavement in Psychoanalytic Theory." *Psychoanalytic Psychology* 13:547–66.

Shelby, D. 1993. "Mourning Theory Reconsidered." In A. Goldberg, ed., *Progress in Self Psychology*, vol. 9, 169–90. Hillsdale, N.J.: Analytic Press.

———. 1994. "Mourning within a Culture of Mourning." In S. A. Cadwell, R. A. Burnham, & M. Forstein, eds., *Therapists on the Front Line: Psychotherapy with Gay Men in the Age of AIDS*, 53–80. Washington, D.C.: American Psychiatric Press.

Silver, R., & C. Wortman. 1980. "Coping with Undesirable Life Events." In J. Garber & M. E. P. Seligman, eds., *Human Helplessness: Theory and Applications*, 279–340. New York: Academic Press.

Slade, A. 1999. "Attachment Theory and Research: Implications for the Theory and Practice of Individual Psychotherapy with Adults." In Cassidy & Shaver 1999, 575–94.

Smith, J. E. 1968. *Experience and God*. New York: Oxford University Press.

Smith, S. 2006. "Poverty Traps: Why the Poor Stay Poor." *World Ark*, July–August, 7–15.

Smith, T. B., M. E. McCullough, & J. Poll. 2003. "Religiousness and Depression: Evidence for a Main Effect and the Moderating Influence of Stressful Life Events." *Psychological Bulletin* 129:614–36.

Sophocles. *The Oedipus Cycle*. 1977. Translated by Dudley Fitts and Robert Fitzgerald. San Diego: Harcourt Brace Jovanovich.

Stone, H. 1991. *The Caring Church: A Guide for Lay Pastoral Care*. Minneapolis: Fortress Press.

Strahan, B. 1991. *Parenting and Religiosity amongst SDA Tertiary Students: An Attachment Theory Approach*. Unpublished manuscript, Avondale College, Cooranbong, New South Wales, Australia.

Stroebe, M., & H. Schut. 1999. "The Dual Process Model of Coping with Bereavement: Rationale and Description." *Death Studies* 23:197–224.

———. 2001. "Models of Coping with Bereavement: A Review." In Stroebe, Hansson, Stroebe, & Schut 2001a, 375–403.

———. 2005. "To Continue or Relinquish Bonds: A Review of Consequences for the Bereaved." *Death Studies* 29:477–94.

Stroebe, M. S., R. O. Hansson, W. Stroebe, & H. Schut. 2001a. *Handbook of Bereavement Research: Consequences, Coping, and Care*. Washington, D.C.: American Psychological Association.

———. 2001b. "Introduction: Concepts and Issues in Contemporary Research on Bereavement." In Stroebe, Hansson, Stroebe, & Schut 2001a, 3–22.

Stroebe, M. S., R. O. Hansson, H. Schut, & W. Stroebe. 2008. *Handbook of Bereavement Research and Practice: Advances in Theory and Intervention*. Washington, D.C.: American Psychological Association.

Stroup, G. 1991. "Theology of Narrative or Narrative Theology? A Response to *Why Narrative?*" *Theology Today* 47, no. 4:424–32.

Sunderland, R. 1993. *Getting Through Grief: Caregiving by Congregations.* Nashville: Abingdon.

Switzer, D. K. 1990. "Grief and Loss." In R. J. Hunter, ed., *Dictionary of Pastoral Care and Counseling,* 472–75. Nashville: Abingdon.

Tarakeshwar, N., & K. I. Pargament. 2001. "The Use of Religious Coping in Families of Children with Autism." *Focus on Autism and Other Developmental Disabilities* 6:247–60.

Taylor, H. 1916. *Cicero: A Sketch of His Life and Works.* Chicago: A. C. McClurg & Co.

Ullman, C. 1982. "Change of Mind, Change of Heart: Some Cognitive and Emotional Antecedents of Religious Conversion." *Journal of Personality and Social Psychology* 42:183–92.

"Understanding the Crisis." 2009. World Bank. http://www.worldbank.org/html/extdr/foodprices/, accessed October 20, 2009.

Vandecreek, L., S. Paget, R. Horton, L. Robbins, M. Oettinger, & K. Tai. 2004. "Religious and Nonreligious Coping Methods among Persons with Rheumatoid Arthritis." *Arthritis and Rheumatism* 51:49–55.

VandenBos, G., ed. 2007. *APA Dictionary of Psychology.* Washington, D.C.: American Psychological Association.

Van Doren, M., ed. 1950. *William Wordsworth: Selected Poetry.* New York: Modern Library.

Vaughn, S. B. 2003. "Recovering Grief in the Age of Grief Recovery." *Journal of Pastoral Theology* 13:36–45.

Wachholtz, A., M. Pearce, & H. Koenig. 2007. "Exploring the Relationship between Spirituality, Coping, and Pain." *Journal of Behavioral Medicine* 30:311–18.

Watts, A. 2006. *Eastern Wisdom, Modern Life: Collected Talks: 1960–1969.* Novato, Calif.: New World Library.

Weatherholt, A. 2008. *Breaking the Silence: The Church Responds to Domestic Violence.* Harrisburg, Pa.: Morehouse.

Weiss, R. 2001. "Grief, Bonds, and Relationships." In Stroebe, Hansson, Stroebe, & Schut 2001a, 47–62.

White, M., & D. Epston. 1990. *Narrative Means to Therapeutic Ends.* New York: Norton.

Wicks, R. 2006. *Overcoming Secondary Stress in Medical and Nursing Practice: A Guide to Professional Resilience and Personal Well-Being.* New York: Oxford University Press.

Willimon, W. 2002. "What September 11 Taught Me about Preaching." In J. Taylor & M. Schwartzentruber, eds., *In the Aftermath: What September 11*

Is Teaching Us about Our World, Our Faith and Ourselves, 103–13. Kelowna, British Columbia, Canada: Northstone.

Wink, P., & M. Dillon. 2001. "Religious Involvement and Health Outcomes in Late Adulthood." In T. G. Plante & A. C. Sherman, eds., *Faith and Health*, 75–106. New York: Guilford.

Wolterstorff, N. 1987. *Lament for a Son*. Grand Rapids: Eerdmans.

Worden, J. W. 2009. *Grief Counseling and Grief Therapy: A Handbook for the Mental Health Practitioner*. 4th ed. New York: Springer.

Wortman, C. B., & R. C. Silver. 1989. "The Myths of Coping with Loss." *Journal of Consulting and Clinical Psychology* 57:349–57.

Wray, T. J. 2003. *Surviving the Death of a Sibling*. New York: Three Rivers.

Yutang, L., ed. 1942. *The Wisdom of China and India*. New York: Random House.

Notes

Introduction

1. See, e.g., Attig 1996, 2001; Neimeyer, 2001a.

2. In their classic grief text, Mitchell and Anderson (1983) propose some general dynamics, elements, and characteristics of grief that may be manifest, the particularity of one's grief notwithstanding.

Chapter 1: Contemporary Topics in Grief

1. "Poverty: At a Glance," 2009.

2. "Understanding the Crisis," 2009.

3. "Fast Facts," 2006.

4. Ibid.

5. See, e.g., Cook & Oltjenbruns 1998; Parkes 1993; Worden 2009.

6. e.g., Freud 1957 [1917]; Lindemann 1944.

7. See, e.g., Field 2006; Field, Gao, & Paderna 2005; Klass & Goss 1999; Stroebe & Schut 2005.

8. See, e.g., Jones 2001; Wicks 2006.

9. See also Sunderland 1993.

10. Such programs are described in Howe 2000 and Stone 1991.

11. Excellent sources of background and information on the Zeugma mosaics and the efforts to excavate them are Basgelen & Ergec 2000 and de Buzareingues, Jones, & Arledge 2000. Also see www.pbs.org/wgbh/nova/zeugma/.

Chapter 2: The History of Grief Theory

1. The use of the English words *grief* and *grieve* to convey the original meaning of related ancient Greek, Latin, and Hebrew words in these translated passages is open to scholarly debate. For the purposes of illustration in this book, it seems appropriate to accept that some translators of these passages do believe that *grief* and *grieve* capture something of what the original authors intended.

2. The quotations in this section are from the following sources: Sophocles 1977, 208; Grene & Lattimore 1956, 328–29; Ovid 1975, 119; Taylor 1916, 599; Shakespeare 1968, 70; Shakespeare 1984, 143; Dickinson 1925, 61.

3. Hagman makes particular mention of Gaines 1997; Hagman 1993, 1995a, 1995b, 1996a, 1996b; Kaplan 1995; Shane & Shane 1990; Shapiro 1996; Shelby 1993, 1994.

4. See, e.g., Calhoun & Tedeschi 2001; Park & Cohen 1993; Park, Cohen, & Murch 1996.

5. See, e.g., Field 2006; Field, Gao, & Paderna 2005; Klass & Goss 1999; Stroebe & Schut 2005.

6. Some subjects also demonstrated a sixth feature, which was taking on some of the behaviors or characteristics of the deceased person.

7. See, e.g., Neimeyer, 2001c; Wortman & Silver 1989.

Chapter 3: Attachment Theory and Attachment to God

1. Most of the theoretical presentation of attachment theory and attachment to God was previously published in Kelley 2009.

2. The additional classification of "disorganized/disoriented" has since been added (Main & Solomon 1986, 1990).

3. Main and Goldwyn (1984, 1998) reported patterns of adult mental representations that seemed to be analogous to behavioral patterns of infants observed by Ainsworth and others (Slade 1999), and the terms they introduced are now commonly used in research on adult attachment. An adult style described as secure or autonomous is analogous to a secure style of attachment among infants. An adult style described as preoccupied is analogous to an anxious-ambivalent style of attachment among infants. An adult style described as dismissing is analogous to an avoidant style of attachment among infants.

4. See, e.g., Haun 1977; Loveland 1968.

5. Kirkpatrick & Shaver 1992; Strahan 1991.

6. See, e.g., Jubis 1991; Potvin 1977.

7. See Lambert, Triandis, & Wolf 1959; Rohner 1975.

8. Kirkpatrick (2005) provides some preliminary data that those with an anxious-ambivalent style of human attachment are most likely to seek out God as a compensatory attachment figure because they crave more closeness than they are getting in their human attachment relationships, whereas those with an avoidant style of human attachment, by definition, are not actively seeking greater connection or closeness to others.

9. See, e.g., Deutsch 1975; Galanter 1979; Ullman 1982.

10. See Miner 2007. I would also offer the following critiques of Kirkpatrick's work. First, his various descriptions of relationship with God seem to limit love for God to something permanently steeped in the childish. "Psychologically, I suggest, a worshiper's love for God is more akin to a child's love for her mother or father than to an adult's love for a romantic

partner or spouse. . . . It is 'attachment-love,' if you will" (2005, 77–79). This perspective does not seem to allow for a relationship with God that has moved, over time, toward greater maturity and even a sense within a person of living and working in some sort of deep intimacy or partnership with God. On a related note, his concept of religiousness is narrowly defined at times. It would be interesting to bring Kirkpatrick's work on attachment to God into dialogue with work on spirituality, faith development, and mysticism. Also, Kirkpatrick's research has involved mostly Christian subjects. A wider range of subjects would strengthen his findings.

11. The formation of lay pastoral caregivers is described by Howe 2000 and Stone 1991.

Chapter 4: Meaning-Making after Loss

1. See, e.g., Attig 1996, 2001; Neimeyer 1999, 2001a; Neimeyer & Keesee 1998.

2. See Augsburger 1986; Polkinghorne 1988.

3. In the last thirty years or so, narrative has become an important focus in a vast array of disciplines, such as literary criticism, history, anthropology, medical ethics, and sociology. Both theology and psychology have also experienced a "narrative turn" (Josselson 2007, 5). Narrative theology encompasses a great many strands and emphases (Stroup 1991). A full treatment of narrative as understood in these disciplines is well beyond the scope of this chapter. I offer a slice of work on narrative specifically as it is understood in the contemporary secular grief field, with emphasis on how to consider this work ministerially.

4. Many authors (e.g., Lester 1995; McAdams 1993; Neimeyer 2000, 2005; Neimeyer, Prigerson, & Davies 2002; Polkinghorne 1988) consider various elements of stories in their work on narrative.

5. This popular quote is often attributed to Anaïs Nin or to the Talmud, but its precise source appears undetermined.

6. See, e.g., Parry & Doan 1994; White & Epston 1990.

7. For excellent reflection on the critical topics of abuse, domestic violence, and the church, see Adams & Fortune 1996; Fortune 1987; Weatherholt 2008. Also consult the fine work of The Faith Trust Institute, www.faithtrustinstitute.org.

8. See, e.g., Attig 2001; Richards 2001.

Chapter 5: Grief, Stress, and Religious Coping

1. See Vaughn 2003; Wolterstorff 1987.

2. Carmichael 2009.

3. Martin 2008.

4. Komaroff 2009.

5. Price, Choi, & Vinokur 2002.

6. Miller 2007b.

7. Shaha & Loeterman 2009.

8. Calhoun & Tedeschi 2001; Schaefer & Moos 1992.

9. See, e.g., Kim, Sherman, & Taylor 2008; Price, Choi, & Vinokur 2002.

10. See, e.g., Marty 1983; and Vaughn 2003.

11. See, e.g., Gass 1987; Jenkins & Pargament 1988; Pargament 1997; Pargament & Abu Raiya 2007; Pargament et al. 1990; Pargament, Koenig, & Perez 2000; Pargament, Smith, Koenig, & Perez 1998; Park & Cohen 1993; Wachholtz, Pearce, & Koenig 2007.

12. Tarakeshwar & Pargament 2001.

13. Mattis, Fontenot, & Hatcher-Kay 2003.

14. Smith, McCullough, & Poll 2003.

15. Pargament, Koenig, Tarakeshwar, & Hahn 2004.

16. Wachholtz, Pearce, & Koenig 2007.

17. Ano & Vasconcelles 2005; Cole 2005; McConnell et al. 2006; Smith, McCullough, & Poll 2003; Vandecreek et al. 2004.

18. Wachholtz, Pearce, & Koenig 2007.

19. Pargament, Koenig, Tarakeshwar, & Hahn 2001.

20. Pargament 1997.

21. Cook & Wimberly 1983.

22. Wachholtz et al. 2007.

23. Pargament underscores that some religious struggle is part and parcel of the spiritual journey, and such struggle may often lead to great growth in "wisdom, maturity, and a sense of connectedness with the transcendent" (Pargament, Murray-Swank, Magyar, & Ano 2005, 257). However, this is clearly not always the result. "Though spiritual struggles may lead to growth, they are not always a prelude to greater well-being, for struggles may also presage pain and decline" (Pargament 2007, 115). Connections to supportive others who can help people to resolve their religious or spiritual struggles seem to be an important factor in the outcome of the struggles (Pargament et al., 2005).

24. See, e.g., Bhui et al. 2008; Cinnirella & Loewenthal 1999; Loewenthal & Cinnirella 1999; Loewenthal, Cinnirella, Evdoka, & Murphy 2001; Pargament & Abu Raiya 2007.

25. Angie and Tom may also find it very helpful to connect with The Compassionate Friends, the national association for parents who have experienced the death of a child. The Compassionate Friends has chapter meetings around the country. Further information is available at www.compassionatefriends.org or by calling 877-969-0010.

Chapter 6: Grief in Relational Perspective

1. Ainsworth 1985; Bowlby 1969, 1973, 1980, 1988.

2. Doka 1989, 2002, 2008.

3. Thomas Attig has worked with the metaphor of grief as a "breaking through" to deeper understanding in a presentation entitled "Brokenness: Reflections on Suffering and Resilience" (Association for Death Education and Counseling, Tampa, Florida, Spring 2006).

4. All page references for Julian's words are with reference to the translation by Colledge and Walsh.

5. I draw the reader's attention to the fine work by Jane Maynard (2006), *Transfiguring Loss: Julian of Norwich as a Guide for Survivors of Traumatic Grief*. Maynard considers Julian as herself a possible survivor of traumatic loss. She then presents Julian's theology and spirituality as a resource for transfiguring loss among those who have survived traumas such as the terrorist attacks of September 11, 2001, the deadly tsunami in Southeast Asia in 2004, and Hurricane Katrina in 2005.

Index of Subjects and Names

Index of Biblical References